For a Few Canards More

For a Few Canards More

Counter Inquiry on Stalin and the Soviet Union

Aymeric Monville

Originally published as *Et Pour Quelques Bobards de Plus: Contre-Enquête sur Staline at l'Union Soviétique* © Editions Delga 2020

WWW.ISKRABOOKS.ORG
US | England | Ireland

Iskra Books is a non-profit, independent, scholarly publisher—publishing original works of revolutionary theory, history, education, and art, as well as edited collections, new translations, and critical republications of older works.

ISBN-13: 979-8-3302-6209-0 (Softcover)

British Library Cataloguing in Publication Data
A catalogue record for this book is available from the British Library

Library of Congress Cataloguing-in-Publication Data
A catalog record for this book is available from the Library of Congress

Cover Art and Design by Ben Stahnke
Editing, Proofing, and Typesetting by David Peat

Contents

The USSR, Lies, and Videotape

The history of the Soviet Union—if it still deserves the name of history—is characterized in France by the absence of debate. The political consensus dictates that the right wing attacks Stalin for being the embodiment or representative of any socialist system, and the left wing condemns him for having distorted noble ideals.

Propaganda operations follow one after the other in an undisturbed manner in the form of horror movie narratives, from *The Red Tyrant* to *Mr. Jones*, passing through to the execrable *Apocalypse: Stalin*.[1] Reputable historians participate in these sinister botches, which are then recommended for teaching, and so on.

The current revival on a massive scale of the old "hoaxes" spread during the Cold War clearly aims at excluding communists from the public space and is inseparable from a hardening class struggle. However, this phenomenon contradicts the current trend, linked to the opening of the archives of the USSR, which dismisses a certain number of black legends.

This book has evolved from a kind of logbook of an editor who has been committed for fifteen years to the creation of a corpus reflecting re-

1 **Ed. Note:** *Le Tyran Rouge [The Red Tyrant]* & *Apocalypse: Staline* [*Apocalypse: Stalin*] were French television documentaries released in 2007 & 2015 respectively. *L'Ombre de Staline* [Released in English as *Mr. Jones*] was a 2019 Polish-Ukrainian-British produced biographical film about Gareth Jones, a journalist who is credited with bringing information about the Ukrainian famine of the 1930s to the non-Communist world.

cent research on the history of the USSR.[2] While compiling these mainly polemical interventions, I was able to benefit from the perspectives and sometimes the advice of research friends, many of whom are quoted in and commented on in this book. I dare to think that this privileged environment is what makes this more than just a militant book, as is sometimes said with disdain. I hope it is, at the very least, a gateway to a broader literature.

The modest goal I have set myself is essentially to conduct a counter-investigation. This should be the job of press commentators but evidently this does not seem to be possible for our contemporary 'Fourth Estate'. It is not intended to supplant the work of historians, but to differentiate between those who work with the sources—especially in Russian, but not only—and those who do not.

Given the urgency, I admit that it has been difficult for me to detach myself from a sometimes biased tone. However, at a time when the European Parliament no longer hesitates to decree an equivalence between Nazism and Communism, as it did in September 2019, would it not be more appropriate to question any such apparent "impartiality," essentially an indifference as to whether Hitler won or not in 1945?

Indeed, whether we like it or not, 1991 does not erase 1945. The disappearance of the USSR has not erased the achievements of the victory of the world over fascism, a victory of which the Soviets were the "soul" and driving force. Therefore, there is no shame in this first experience of socialism (after the Paris Commune) whose historical balance has consisted in engendering a world where racism is a despised thing, where war is no longer a positive value, and where colonialism, at least in its official form, is past history. What the USSR represented is a reality that is still present and deserves to be defended.

To conclude, a few words in response to a common objection which, at first glance, may seem well-intentioned. Some argue that it would be counterproductive to revisit the figure of Stalin, since the conditions under which we will one day achieve socialism will surely not have the tragic character that characterized the USSR in the midst of its siege. Of course, debates need not be battlefields, not everything is either defensible or attackable, and I in no way share the fundamentals of this, shall we say, "Schmittian" worldview, where every political consideration is marked by a friends/enemies confrontation. My perspective as an ordi-

---

2 See "Works Cited," p. 77.

nary Marxist is that of humanity reconciled through labor and reason. Nevertheless, should we exclude the simple idea expressed by the rather un-Marxist Julien Freund, which is that sometimes, whether we like it or not, in politics, "it is the enemy who designates you"?

The fact is this invasive propaganda is a hunt for a man, for the "red" man, that takes shape. So let us not be naive. In our era, when neo-Banderite propaganda is even in our neighborhood cinemas, and state anti-communism is brainwashing our children, not knowing what to say about Stalin becomes cowardice. No one is asking for the return of the cult of personality, but to continue to pass over everything there was and will be about the Stalinist era while one claims to be a Marxist is to fall short of Marx's thinking. Indeed, he would not have stood for the idea that the liberation of the workers and peoples could so easily be spared a phase of dictatorship of the proletariat.

Aymeric Monville
July 2020

Note for the Second Edition

In addition to the corrections of expression that we owe to Sophie's vigilance (thanks again), this second [French] edition consisted in replacing [...] an interview on Soviet historiography dating from 2016 by a more updated answer, motivated by the publication of the French version of the Dewey Commission report, and also by the analysis made of it in an Italian book soon to be published **[Ed. Note:** volume published in 2021] by Delga editions, *Le Vol de Piatakov. La collaboration tactique entre Trotsky et les nazis* [*Piatakov's Flight. The tactical collaboration between Trotsky and the nazis*], by D. Burgio, M. Leoni and R. Sidoli.

A. M.
December 2020

Note for the First English Edition

Additional contextual information is provided throughout the text by footnotes beginning as "**Ed. Note**." All other footnotes, including citations styles, have been preserved from the original text.

D.P.
February 2024

A Simple Criticism or a Virulent Reprobation?

About the documentary *Goulag, une histoire soviétique* [*Gulag: A Soviet History*][1]

We have watched the nearly three hours of ARTE's documentary on the gulag, first of all because communists should not look the other way. This story is not about a distant country, but about what was, for a long time, the second homeland of any consistent progressive and anti-fascist: the USSR. This country was born out of the rejection of imperialist butchery. It is the first socialist country in history and the main victor over Hitler. It sent a signal of revolt to many colonized peoples, it put an end to Nazi barbarism, but it also experienced very dark pages and forms of social organization unconsciously derived from centuries of capitalist oppression. For many years, the capitalist encirclement of the USSR, and later that of the socialist camp, did not allow this "withering away of the state" envisioned by the classics of Marxism to take place (the initial dictatorship of the proletariat gradually giving way the overall social self-management characteristic of completed com-

1 By P. Rotman, N. Werth and F. Aymé, February 2020.

munism). On the contrary, this siege provoked the need to reinforce the State apparatus, with its charge of undertaking a forced industrial development in a hyper-centralized way and prioritizing the military capacities indispensable to face fascism (in almost all Western Europe, but also with Japan on the eastern flank of the USSR), and continuing with the American threat, which showed in Hiroshima that there was a risk of nuclear extermination of the USSR and the whole of humanity (the "better dead than red" of the Western reactionaries did not refer only to the USSR, and took the whole of humanity hostage).

We must recognize it, and we do recognize it. On the other hand, we cannot remain silent in the face of a certain number of assertions, omissions, and manipulations in this documentary, co-written, among others, by one of the authors of the *Black Book of Communism*. The millions of deaths from communism do not correspond to the deaths in the gulag camps (1.6 million, of which 900,000 in wartime) nor to those of the Great Purge (700,000 dead), but instead refer to the death inflicted on the communists (27 million victims during the Second World War). This is a point of comparison that is never addressed in the documentary. That is also why the scandalous amalgamation between Nazism and communism, in addition to being factually untenable, is politically criminal in these times of fascist tendencies and deceitfully forgetful of the close link between capitalism and fascism, it is also morally repugnant.

***

First of all, we note that this documentary is financed by a European fund (Creative Europe, media of the European Union), at the same time that the European Parliament, aligning itself with Poland, the Baltic countries, and Ukraine, intends to ban all communist activity, motivated by a sinister comparison between Nazism and communism, which is only possible with base misrepresentations and by hiding the responsibilities of capital in the emergence of fascism.

The tone of the documentary leaves no doubt about the profound harmony with the anti-communist repression we are living through, when they say, for example, about Stalin in 1945: "Strange paradox, the bloodthirsty dictator stands alongside the democracies as the architect of the victory over Nazi totalitarianism."

We understand: for the authors of the gulag documentary, on one side, there are the totalitarian regimes (Nazi and Stalinist), and on the other side, the "democracies," as if the latter, also on the path to fascism (including in France despite the very temporary halt by the Popular Front), had not encouraged the Nazis—from the "non-intervention" in Spain (to the detriment of the Republicans) to the "choice of defeat" in 1940, including Munich and many other "good manners" towards Hitler, Franco, and Mussolini.

However, what this documentary shows are labor camps, extremely harsh, sometimes dreadful, an exploitation for which we have had numerous equivalents in the West, both on its soil and in its colonies. However, they are in no way comparable to the extermination camps set up by the Nazis. Anne Applebaum, correspondent for *The Economist*, author of a book on the gulag, and an authority in American neoconservative spheres, says herself, very clearly, that these camps were not intended to kill.[2]

Tell the Whole Truth

According to the documentary, about 20 million people passed through the gulags. Anne Applebaum speaks of 18 million, while Nicolas Werth speaks of 15 million in his latest book, *Le Cimetière de l'espérance* [*The Cemetery of Hope*], even though he is co-author of this same documentary. These figures are very high. They must also be put in context. The gulag never had more than 2,561,351 prisoners per year (1950 figure), which implies that not all of them were sentenced to severe penalties and that many were released from the gulag. Likewise, Nicolas Werth states in the same book that on January 1, 1940, 60.7% of the detainees were serving sentences of less than five years.

Most importantly, what this documentary remains silent on is the number of deaths recorded in the gulag. Indeed, as terrible as these shattered destinies were, they fall far short of the figures in the usual Cold War propaganda. In reality, 1.6 million people died in the gulag. Another fact that the documentary knowingly conceals is that most of these deaths (about 900,000) took place during the Second World War, in obviously exceptional circumstances. Indeed, at a time when the country was fighting for its collective survival, the Soviet Union suffered the loss of 27 million of its fellow citizens under the slogan "All for the Front, All for Victory!" In the gulags, this resulted in the deaths of 115,484

2 *Cf.* the appendix to Applebaum's book, *Gulag: A History*.

people in 1941, 352,560 in 1942 (at the height of the total war led by Nazi Germany and the heroic Soviet resistance), 267,826 in 1943 (the last year of the Battle of Stalingrad and the Battle of Kursk), 114,481 in 1944 and 81,917 in 1945; that is 932,267 out of a total of 1,606,748 for the period 1930-1956.[3]

Another "Forgotten" Documentary

Of course, the documentary does mention very high mortality in the gulag construction works. I have noted all the occurrences:

1. "The detainees literally work themselves to death. This planned death serves the needs of social, political, and ethnic cleansing decided by the Soviet power."
2. "12,000 people die on the White Sea-Baltic Sea canal construction site, i.e. 10% of the workforce."
3. "In the Kolyma camps, the mortality rate reached 10% per year between 1937 and 1938."
4. On the Moscow-Volga canal: "At its peak, about 200,000 detainees work at the construction site, 30,000 lose their lives."
5. On the construction of the Second Trans-Siberian Railway (Baikal-Amur line): "At the end of the 1930s, the construction site exploited the labor of nearly 200,000 detainees, 10,000 of whom lost their lives, i.e. one death every 150 meters."

In his book on Stalin, in which he comments on figures similar to those advanced by historian Stephen Kotkin, Grover Furr clearly shows that the essential information is never given: most of these deaths occurred between 1932 and 1933, i.e. during the years of the typhus epidemic and famine, the latter of which, contrary to what Ukrainian nationalists say, did not only affect Ukraine.[4]

Indeed, of the 12,318 deaths recorded at the Belomor (Baltic Sea-White Sea) canal construction site, 8,870 occurred in the year 1933 (1,438 in 1931, 2010 in 1932).[5]

---

3 Figures reported by A. Applebaum.

4 **Ed Note:** The book referenced is published in English under the title *Stalin. Waiting For... The Truth! Exposing the Falsehoods in Stephen Kotkin's 'Stalin. Waiting for Hitler, 1929-1941*, published by Red Star Publishers, 2019.

5 1. A.I. Kokurin, Yu. N. Morukov (dir.), *Stalinskie Stroïki GULAGA 1930-*

Clearly, Stephen Kotkin applies the same methods as those of the gulag documentary, since he dares to write the following in his book Stalin: Waiting for Hitler 1929-1941:

> More than 126,000 forced laborers did the work, almost entirely without machines, and probably at least 12,000 died doing so, while orchestras played in the background.[6]

For his part, Grover Furr, in his book on Stalin, conceived as an anti-Kotkin, states:

> Therefore, the prisoners did not die "doing that," i.e. because of mediocre or brutal working conditions. They died of starvation, disease and other natural causes. The orchestras were part of the cultural and educational programs for prisoners. I have not found similar cultural activities for American prisoners at that time. In fact, the brutal conditions and high mortality in the "chain gangs" in the United States was a major problem at that time. The same is true when we compare the horrific—indeed, fascist—abuses and murders of early black workers in the United States after the Civil War, which Douglas Blackmon discusses.[7]

In his same forthcoming book, Grover Furr reports the following about the workers on the Moscow-Volga Canal:

Kotkin writes:

> On April 22, Stalin paid his third visit to a part of the eighty-mile canal linking the Moscow and Volga rivers [...] The canal was built by gulag laborers, more than 20,000 of whom likely perished.

No evidence is given for this statement. Note the word *likely*! Kotkin doesn't know the number but puts one in anyway.

The primary source for this kind of information is A.I. Kokurin, IU. N Morukov, eds. *Stalinskie Stroiki GULAGA 1930-1953*. Dokumenty. [*Stalinist GULAG Construction*].[8] The mortality figures cited here are not for canal workers but for the "Dmitlag" camp as a whole. The total of deaths recorded in the camp between September 14, 1932, and January 31, 1938, is 22,842.

1953. Dokumenty. Moscow, MDF — "Materik," 2005, pp. 33-34.

6 **Ed. Note:** Published in English by Penguin Press, 2017.

7 Douglas Blackmon, *Slavery By Another Name. The Re-enslavement of Black Americans from the Civil War to World War II*, New York, Anchor Books, Random House, 2008 (see also the excellent website at http://www.slaverybyanothername.com/).

8 Moscow: MDF — "Materik" 2005, pp. 30-102.

By far the highest number of deaths—39% of the total—is recorded for 1933—8873. This was the year of famine in much of the USSR, and also of serious typhus. There was a severely elevated death rate throughout the Soviet Union during these same years. Omitting this information gives the impression that these people were "worked to death" or died from poor conditions.

But that is not the case. According to the same source the working day was 10 hours long. Breakfast lasted 45 minutes, dinner two hours, and three hours in the evening were devoted to cultural and educational activities. These were better conditions than existed for millions of workers in the capitalist world, to say nothing of the colonies of the Western imperialist countries. And far better than for prisoners in the prisons of the West. Even Kokourine and Moroukov, staunch anticommunists from the "Memorial" society, include this information. Kotkin does not!

Inconvenient Comparisons

It would then be necessary to compare these figures with those of other construction works in the capitalist field. For example, the excavation of the Panama Canal also caused 22,000 victims, and in this case we are talking about wage labor, not prison labor. As for the railroads of the colonial countries, the deaths are also counted in deaths per meter of construction site. Between 1921 and 1934, the construction of the Congo-Ocean line (linking Brazzaville to Pointe-Noire) cost the lives of 17,000 people, exploited and dehumanized by the colonizing logic.[9] These figures are therefore of the same order of magnitude. As for the forced labor imposed by colonialism, individuals were beaten on the basis of their indigenous status, without having been convicted by any court (however much these convictions may be questioned).

One can certainly regret that the USSR did not manage to escape the type of forced economic development that the capitalist West also experienced, perhaps due to the dreadful encirclement context and the necessity to overcome the underdevelopment of the *Ancien Regime* to transform the country into an industrial power capable of competing with capitalist and/or fascist powers.

9 Source: *La ligne Congo-Océan: Une traverse, un mort, GEO,* published 20/05/2016, https://www.geo.fr/voyage/l-afrique-au-temps-des-colonies-la-ligne-congo-ocean-une-traverse-un-mort-161171.

The capitalist West, on the other hand, did not have the excuse of enduring a war for its survival, had several centuries to industrialize and had at its disposal the human and natural resources of ruthlessly plundered colonies (how many millions of deaths among Africans, South Americans, North American Indigenous peoples, Asians?).

Therefore, the amalgamation with Nazism and its extermination camps, its genocides, its Shoah, and the master race who intended to enslave entire peoples they had decreed as "inferior" is not valid, even more so when it serves to mask the fact that fascism was nothing more than a stage of the development of capitalism, its most savage part, while "ordinary" imperialism continued to exterminate invisibly through its colonial wars and, behind it, the "invisible" daily pillage.

At the height of the gulag system, 2.7 million prisoners is, however, a scandal from a humane perspective. What seems even more scandalous within this scandal is the fact that the number of convictions significantly increased after the war, only to plateau around 1950. The influx of prisoners of war, the temporary abolition of the death penalty from 1947 to 1950, and the fact that the USSR was experiencing only an armed "peace" at that time do not explain everything. Still, I recall that the USSR put a definitive end to the gulag, while in the United States—which has historically been involved in the persecution of "reds," African-American, and feminist activists, etc., in other words, a fully acknowledged political repression—the prison population was 2.3 million people in 2010, which is approximately the same number of people as the gulag at its height. In both cases, these very abnormal figures can be explained by the national particularities and the excessively violent history of these two countries, Russia and the United States.

Although, if it is a question of comparing systems, we note that the gulag labor camps did not last more than twenty years, which were terrible years for the USSR since it had to face attempts of internal subversion constantly, while triumphant capitalism does not count at all on improving its social regulation by means of imprisonment. On the contrary, it leads us to another world war: since the disappearance of the USSR, the planet has never been worse and the bourgeois states tending to fascization are more and more numerous, especially in the United States (with the Patriot Act), where there has been an institutional return of torture (Guantanamo, undignified treatment of Palestinian prisoners, etc.), and with the use of hunger as a weapon against entire peoples (US embargoes and blockades). In any case, persecuting communists will not improve their lot.

WALL STREET NEED NOT DESPAIR

This is for the gulag. The gulag was not meant to kill, although no one claims that there were no political executions under Stalin. In fact, we know the precise figure for death sentences: 786,098 from 1934 to 1953, most in the years 1937 and 1938. This figure is also cited by Anne Applebaum and emanates from a 1993 article written in English by Zemskov, Getty and Rittersporn, well known to researchers.[10]

In this case, Anne Applebaum again feels obliged, after having quoted these figures, to add, without logic, "in fact, we will never really know," a procedure that certainly permits her to not disappoint Wall Street and her public who surely expected more. It is nevertheless necessary to acknowledge that here too, in the absence of being publicized, the figure is widely accepted.

It does send shivers down the spine, especially when we see that most of the executions are concentrated in the years 1937 and 1938. However, the reason why this figure is little known, even today, is that it invalidates the propaganda of Medvedev, Conquest, Solzhenitsyn, and company, each citing millions of dead. The historical causes of the "Great Purge" are the subject of historiographical debate, which is far from over. In his interviews with Felix Tchouev,[11] Molotov justifies these executions by a Machiavellian will to nip in the bud any hint of a fifth column; but the Stalinist authorities had rather insisted on Yezhov's treason as the main cause of the execution of numerous innocents (hence the term *Yezhovshchina* to characterize the period). For their part, the work of American historians, in particular John Archibald Getty, highlighted the fact that the desire for repression and control also originated from the grassroots to punish bureaucratic incompetence. Undoubtedly, the war in Spain and Hitler's rise to power had created a feeling of widespread distrust in the USSR, all the more so when Hitler, quickly recognized by the "Western democracies," openly promised slavery, and even the extermination

10 J. A. GETTY, G. T. RITTERSPORN, and V. N. ZEMSKOV, "Les victimes de la répression pénale dans l'URSS d'avant-guerre" [The Victims of Penal Repression in the Prewar USSR], *Revue des études slaves*, 65 (1993), pp. 631-670.

11 Félix TCHOUEV, *Conversations avec Molotov: 140 entretiens avec le bras droit de Staline* [*Conversations with Molotov: 140 interviews with Stalin's right-hand man*], Albin Michel, Paris, 1995.

of the Slavs and other "subhumans," in *Mein Kampf*. In this case, the analogy that comes to mind would be the reaction of the Parisian population, threatened with extermination by the Brunswick Manifesto of the summer of 1792 and which, combined with the defeats of the then ill-prepared French army (by Louis XVI's own confession, who voluntarily declared war on Austria in order to lose it and thus crush the French Revolution), favored the massacres of September 1792. Danton, long before Robespierre, wanted to give these proceedings at least a legal procedural form.

In any case, it is worth considering that the USSR was already under attack at the end of 1917, by a coalition of at least fourteen capitalist countries (headed by the United States, France, the United Kingdom, Japan and Germany). It went on to face a war of extermination arraigned against it, which cost it 27 million civilian and military losses, even though it emerged victorious from the conflict. Therefore, the question according to which such a state could dispense with a political police and a policy that claimed to be in a certain way a "dictatorship of public safety" is not intellectually illegitimate as a hypothesis, but remains mainly rhetorical.

It is necessary to take into consideration this mental context if we want to try to understand a minimum of what happened, and not analogies with contexts of genocidal extermination coldly planned as such, as the Nazis committed with the Jews and the Romani people (6 million dead), or those committed by other colonial or imperialist powers: total genocides (such as the against the inhabitants of Tasmania by the British) or quasi-total genocides (such as in the cases of the Armenians, and Indigenous North American peoples who, "until around 1890," were "massacred in genocidal proportions").[12]

In a similar vein of "manipulation," another typical Cold War technique involved playing with words, suggesting, for example, that Soviet authorities, unable to have a nationality that had massively collaborated with the Nazis in the rear of the Red Army, had "deported" the Crimean Tatars, with the insinuation of homicide that the term "deportation" conveys in the West due to the Jewish deportations to death camps. The reality is that, of the 151,720 Crimean Tatars sent to the Uzbek Soviet Socialist Republic in May 1944, 191 people (0.13%) died during trans-

---

12 *Cf.* Pap Ndiaye, "L'extermination des Indiens d'Amérique du Nord" [The Extermination of the Indians of North America], *in* Marc Ferro (dir.), *Le Livre noir du colonialisme* [*The Black Book of Colonialism*], Paris, Robert Laffont, 2003, p. 89.

port, as reported by Viktor Zemskov, who is, let us remember, Anne Applebaum's main source.[13]

An Unacceptable Lack of Clarity in Historical Research

If the statistics on the gulag are not challenged, why then is it not possible to have access to accurate information? Readers of the Russian Wikipedia page on the gulag, which is expected to convey the common opinion, can read statistics of gulag deaths, year after year. The figure of 1.6 million dead is the only one provided, since no one disputes it. The reference given is this: ГУЛАГ (Главное управление лагерей). 1918-1960. Глава III // Составители: А. И. Кокурин, Н. В. Петров.—МФД, 2000.

More evasive, the French Wikipedia page limits itself to saying "between one and two million people did not survive" without indicating any source, which constitutes a real lie by omission since we do have statistics. This lack of clarity undoubtedly authorizes *La Croix*, which broadcasts Patrick Rotman's documentary, to speak of "4 million dead" from the gulag; *Paris Match*, speaks of "several million," and so on. It is clear that in the country of the "Black Book" it is not so easy to renounce the propaganda of the "millions of dead."

As for Anne Applebaum, she declares herself "reluctant" to use statistics; Werth, in her latest book, rounds Zemskov's 1.6 million to 2 million, no one knows why. And this documentary concludes with an elusive "millions dead." One also recalls Solzhenitsyn's 110 million, and Roy Medvedev's 40 million. At this level, it is no longer history, but instead it is war propaganda that had already started with a book entitled Mein Kampf.

In reality, we see that the millions of dead of communism are not those of the gulag, but those inflicted on the communists. Considering these facts, the comparison between Nazism and communism is simply odious. However, ARTE's documentary does not even talk about the 27 million dead. It even has the bad taste to switch from black and white images to color images when it evokes, of all things... the Nazi invasion of the USSR. At the same time, it never talks about the fact that during a very short period, Russia of the Soviet Union had become a great indus-

13 V. N. Zemskov, "К вопросу о масштабах репресссий в СССР," Социологичеческие иссследования, no. 9, 1995, pp. 118-127.

trial and scientific power that most Russians yearn for today. A power that played an important role in the emancipation of women (right to vote granted since 1917, right to divorce by mutual consent, etc.) and in supporting the struggles for decolonization, without forgetting that, without the presence of the socialist camp in the world, the social advances of the Western countries (which Western propaganda magically attributes to the "Glorious Thirties") would have been unthinkable. In fact, quite the opposite has been the case since the fall of the USSR. Can we expect reputable reviewers of the history of World War II to show even an iota of objectivity? They are not even capable of saying, as De Gaulle did in 1944, when he signed in Moscow the Treaty of Mutual Assistance with Stalin: "The French know what Soviet Russia did for them, and they know that it was precisely Soviet Russia that played the leading role in their liberation." It's enough to ask an uncomfortable question for the dominant ideology: would the Jews of Europe not have perished to the last if the Soviet Union had not defeated the Nazis—who concentrated 2/3 of their divisions on the Eastern Front? This simple fact shows the despicable indecency of those who denigrate the first socialist country in history—with the terrible distortions inflicted on it by the tragic history of the 20th century—and attenuate the capitalist character of the Third Reich, which was intentionally and methodically exterminatory.

As a Documentary on Stalinist Repression in General

The documentary doesn't talk about it because it would be necessary to stay on topic? Well, actually, the documentary doesn't hesitate—why not?—to recall the entirety of Stalinist repression. But again, we must be precise. In this case, the mention of famines targets a specific political plan: while it was the Communists who eventually put an end to the infernal cycle of famines that Russia was experiencing, and that this necessarily involved the establishment of a planned economy and the right to work for all, it is collectivization, and not its failures and excesses, denounced by Stalin himself, that will be incriminated by the documentary. However, in his article "Stalin, Soviet Culture, and Collectivization," Mark Tauger, an agricultural historian specializing in Russian famines, does not make collectivization the sole cause of the famine of 1931-1933 and shows, on the contrary, the positive aspects of the upheavals in agriculture throughout Soviet history, including the victory in 1945 (which is no small feat given that the country that defeated Hitler was itself devastated: something unknown to the United States, which did not land in Europe until June 1944).

Reference is also made in the documentary to the Katyn massacres. One can only arrive at the version "it was the Soviets who committed this massacre, not the Nazis" by giving credence to the documents handed over by Yeltsin to the Polish government, which notably contains a glaring forgery: a letter from Stalin to Beria dated 1940 with the stamp of the Central Committee of the CPSU, the name of the Communist Party that only came into use from... 1952. One can only arrive at the opposite conclusion by denying the discoveries of the mass grave in Volodymyr-Volynskyi (2011-2012), the site of the massacre of populations from western Ukraine by the SS. Researchers there exhumed two badges of Polish soldiers supposed to have been executed, according to the so-called official version, at... 1,200 kilometers away. This discovery immediately led to the halt of the research by Ukrainian and Polish authorities. One can only arrive at the opposite conclusion by putting faith in the Nazi report, apparently concocted in such haste that it mentions, for example, a letter written in German to a camp director by a Polish soldier, indicating that the Polish prisoners had passed through a Nazi camp before their execution. On this matter, the author of a recent book on Katyn (Grover Furr)—and his humble French publisher (myself)—await staunch critics.[14]

Regarding the "origins" of the gulag, especially the Solovki Islands, it should be noted that the documentary relies on the book by Raymond Duguet, *Un bagne en Russie rouge* [*A Prison in Red Russia*], republished with a preface by Nicolas Werth in 2004. However, historian Jean-Jacques Marie had already discredited this propaganda work and demonstrated that the testimonies of former prisoners contradicted the description of an extermination camp made, from Paris, by the propagandist Duguet.[15]

The USSR, the Only Bulwark against the Terrorist Dictatorship of the Bourgeoisie: Fascism

It will be understood: the current campaign surrounding the gulag, relayed on the European Union's favorite channel, has little to do with le-

14 **Ed. Note:** Furr's "The Mystery of the Katyn Massacre."

15 See https://www.marxists.org/francais/cmo/n23/O_Chronique_6_corr.pdf

gitimate access to scientific information, even when it is uncomfortable for us communists. The European Parliament, through its positions, has not contributed much to raising the debate.

Indeed, through its opinion of September 19, 2019, it aims to establish an equivalence between communism and Nazism and makes the Molotov-Ribbentrop Pact the driving force behind World War II. This crude method allows capitalist forces to be exonerated from their documented funding of fascisms, repeated capitulations to Nazi expansionism, and the Munich-like spirit that animated a significant portion of elites in so-called democratic countries. When the French Minister of Foreign Affairs, Bonnet, said to Ribbentrop in Munich in 1938, "We leave you a free hand in the East," we see, however, a deep collusion between capitalist and colonial powers for the division of the world. Hitler, above all, was a supporter of Anglo-Saxon "white supremacy" and intended to reserve for the Slavs the fate experienced by Native Americans. Faced with this desire to secure for Germany the "place in the sun" already demanded by Wilhelm II, different national bourgeoisies then hesitated between two options:

1. To endorse a colonialist and racist world-sharing plan: roughly, North America controls South America, France controls part of Africa and Indochina, England controls the rest of Africa, as well as India, and Germany carves out its colonial empire in the East. This is the "Munich spirit."
2. To curb German (and Japanese) ambitions, based on the entirely plausible idea that the Munich-like division of the world would ultimately lead to a confrontation between powers equivalent to that of the First World War but on a larger scale. In these conditions, the English colonial empire could not tolerate a German rival. This is the Churchillian spirit.

The European Parliament intends to criminalize the only political force that opposed with all its might, not only the European fascisms (with Nazism at the head), but also any kind of racism or colonialism, and at the same time ignoring that the fascisms and the so-called Western democracies were at times rivals and accomplices (we know, for example, that Churchill praised Mussolini). In view of the facts, the equation Hitler=Stalin, apart from hiding the profound link between Hitler and capitalism, is simply inadmissible, as well as repugnant.

We do not know how many victims the USSR would have had to

mourn if it had lost, not to mention what France would have lost, which Hitler wanted to break up and transform into a country of "bellboys and gardeners." Hitler's statements leave no doubt that the Soviet peoples were doomed to slavery and extermination. In this connection, let us recall that the equation Hitler=Stalin is all the more inadmissible inasmuch as Germany had moreover entered Soviet territory to bring death and desolation there, while the Soviet occupation of the eastern part of Germany created the GDR, i.e., the richest country in COMECON. All this is affirmed by the peoples of the former USSR who lived and "experienced" the two systems in succession, first the socialist and then the capitalist, and this at the same time that the counter-revolutionary regime established by Yeltsin and maintained by Putin through national pride, does not cease to vilify and blacken Lenin and the October Revolution. This in no way means that the Russians, especially the workers and peasants, close their eyes to the unjust and blind repressions, but that they take everything into consideration in the knowledge that history is tragic. The French do the same with the key figures of their history, no less tragic when one looks at it closely, especially for the popular classes and the ex-colonized, so should one condemn the French Revolution, which had great lights as well as tragic shadows? One has only to read Hugo's *Ninety-Three* to see how one can do justice to Danton or Robespierre without applauding the very real outpourings of the Great Terror. Even less so to the counter-revolutionary coalitionists who, at the time, were trying to strangle our country from within and without, not in order to abolish privileges, but to re-establish them.

We have seen: whatever the contortions anti-communists of all kinds employ to disguise history, the desire to establish a link of equivalence between communism and Nazism always breaks down in the face of reality. Incidentally, we are still waiting for a documentary listing the victims of capitalism, which kills every day in monstrous proportions: as Gilles Perrault recalled in his review of the *Black Book of Communism* in *Le Monde diplomatique* of December 1997, what will be the weight of the 40,000 children who, according to UNICEF, die every day of malnutrition in the Third World?

***

Appendix: Undeniable Statistics

To those who doubt the validity of the figures we convey, we point out that we owe this rigorous combing of the archives, after the USSR's dissolution, to Viktor Zemskov, a historian who died in 2015 and to whom Werth pays—at last—tribute in his latest book, although he does not fully endorse it:

> I met with Viktor Zemskov, who explained to me at length the painstaking collation of sources that had enabled him to establish the figures he was proposing, before recommending me to the archivist responsible for the gulag collections, Dina Nokhotovich, who gave me access to part of these documents. From the outset, I realized that the discoveries of my Russian colleagues deserved to be widely disseminated through a foreign history journal accessible to a wide public and I wrote, in 1993, "gulag: the true figures" in *L'Histoire*.

The statistics provided by Zemskov come from the Central State Archive of the Soviet Union (TsAGAOR USSR), now renamed the State Archive of the Russian Federation (GARF). This is where the statistical reports of the OGPU-NKVD-MGB-MVD for the period 1930-1950 are stored.

Zemskov's statements leave no ambiguity about the reliability of the statistics. Below is his response to the polemic with historian Antonov-Ovseyenko:

> The question of forgery could be considered if we were to rely on one or several different documents. However, it is impossible to simulate a complete archive fund located in a state warehouse with thousands of storage units, which also includes a wide range of primary materials. Assuming that these primary materials are fake is only possible by assuming the absurd idea that each camp had two offices: one that did authentic paperwork, and a second that did fake paperwork. [...] The assumption that this documentation might contain underestimated information is untenable, since it was unprofitable and undesirable for the NKVD bodies to underestimate the scope of their activities, otherwise they risked falling out of favor with the authorities for "insufficient activity."[16]

And Zemskov concludes:

> We have absolutely accurate information that during 20 years (from January 1, 1934 to January 1, 1954), 1,053,829 people died in the forced labor camps (ITL) of the gulag. During the period 1939-1951 (no information for 1945), 86,582 people died in the prisons of the USSR. Unfortunately, in the gulag documents we

16 Author's translation from Zemskov's work "Заключеннные, спецпоселенцы, ссыльнопоселеленцы, ссыльные и высланнны. Стататистико-географичеческий аспект," История СССР, 1991, vol. 5, p. 151.

have not been able to find consolidated statistics on mortality in the forced labor colonies (ITK) of the gulag. The fragmentary information we identified allows us to conclude that the mortality rate was lower in ITK than in ITL. Thus, in 1939 it remained at the level of 3.29% of the annual quota in the camps, and at 2.30% in the colonies. This is confirmed by another fact: with an approximately equal number and circulation of departing and arriving prisoners in 1945, 43,848 died in ITL and 37,221 in ITK. In the period 1935-1938, there were approximately 2 times fewer prisoners in ITK than in ITL; in 1939, 3.7 times fewer; in 1940, 4 times fewer; in 1941, 3.5 times fewer; in 1942, almost 4 times fewer; and in 1943, almost 2 times fewer. In the period 1944-1949, the number of prisoners in ITL and ITK was approximately the same; in 1950, in ITL it became 20-25 % higher than in ITK; in 1951, 1.5 times higher; and in 1952-1953, almost 2.5 times higher.

In the period 1935-1953, the colonies contained an average of nearly twice as many prisoners as in the camps and their per capita mortality rate was lower. Using the extrapolation method, it is possible to state with a sufficient degree of confidence that in the colonies from 1935 to 1953, no more than 0.5 million people died. Thus, in the period 1934-1953, between 1.6 and 1.7 million prisoners died in the camps, colonies and prisons. Moreover, this number includes not only "enemies of the people" but also criminals (of whom there were more). The ratio of political prisoners to criminals in the gulag fluctuated at different times quite significantly, but during the 1930s and early 1950s, it was close to the average level of 1 : 3. The data are characteristic of January 1, 1951, when the gulag contained 2,528,146 prisoners, of whom 579,918 were political and 1,948,228 convicted of criminal offenses, i.e., a ratio of 1 : 3.3; in the camps, 1 : 2.2 (475,976 and 1,057,791); and in the colonies, 1 : 8.5 (103,942 and 890,437).

Even taking into account the numerous evidence available in the literature, according to which, the mortality rate among politicians was higher than among criminals, we cannot reduce this ratio below the level of 1 : 2. On the basis of the above statistics, it can be stated that for every politician killed in prison, there were at least two criminals killed."[17]

February 17, 2020

17 Author's translation from Viktor N. Zemskov, "Политические репресссии в СССР (1917-1990 гг.) ," Росссия XXI, 1-2, 1994.

Katyn: When the Lines—and Borders—are Crossed

The ARTE Documentary does not even Acknowledge the Current Russian-Polish Border[1]

By watching this ARTE documentary on Katyn, we were all the more startled, thinking that, like any program on the same channel, there was also a German version. Indeed, judging by what is currently being broadcast in the media during prime time, it is no longer surprising that the far right is currently making such a breakthrough in Germany, as the dominant ideology tells it what it wants to hear.

Obviously, I did not expect this new ARTE documentary to present evidence apt to contradict the official version ("the Soviets did it"), even though there is plenty of it and particularly since the 2011-2012 Volodymyr-Volynskyi excavations, which we will discuss later. Let us simply

---

1 Regarding the documentary *Les Bourreaux de Staline, Katyn 1940* [Stalin's Executioners, Katyn 1940] by Cédric Turba and Olivia Gomolinski, Feb. 2020

note that, as in the previous ARTE documentary dealing with the gulag, the elements of context likely to make us better understand the event or the phenomenon in question are exclusively intra-Soviet.

The gulag and Katyn camps (in their official version, that of Soviet guilt) would be explained by a kind of brutality intrinsic to the regime. However, the context of civil war and fascist threat does not exist.

According to the documentary, the Nazis burst into Soviet history in an unexpected way on June 22, 1941 and this rupture of the Non-Aggression Pact, materialized by the military invasion, is qualified by ARTE as a "plot twist." The Moscow Trials are no longer presented as a bloody deviation in a context of fear in the face of the Nazi sabotage and espionage, which were in fact real. On the contrary, they are described as purely "imaginary." To this day, no one in France has had the idea of qualifying as imaginary what Marc Bloch pointed out about "the strange defeat," and which Annie Lacroix-Riz considerably substantiates in her work *Le choix de la défaite* [*The Choice of Defeat*],[2] namely, the formation of a pro-German fifth column in interwar France. However, at a time when the collaborationists are re-baptized as "vichy-resistants," anything is possible.

This documentary, critical of the NKVD, also finds it necessary to mention that during the war, this organization punished deserters. What does this imply? That it would have been better for the Russian front to be breached when, as we know, it retreated in good order? Unless, in hindsight, ARTE also wished for "the victory of Germany because without it, Bolshevism would establish itself everywhere tomorrow"? We would not dare to believe that.

The Imposed Figures of a Documentary about Stalin

We detect more inconsistencies: the request for the execution of the Polish prisoners, formulated by Beria on March 5, 1940, is presented as part of the continuity of the purges of 1937-1938 and, therefore, it is considered "banal." We are supposed to be in 1940, i.e. two years after the end of the Great Purge and, as is often ignored and also not recalled in the documentary, it was Beria who, by expelling Yezhov, put an end to the era of mass executions.

2 **Ed. Note:** Published by Armand Colin, 2010.

We are also told that the NKVD would have executed the "quasi-totality of the generals of the Red Army."

As opposed to the 50 percent loss rate reported by Cold War historian Robert Conquest, it is necessary to remember that purges in the army affected 7.7% of the military command (nachal sostav) in the worst year (1937) and 3.7% the following year.[3] To conceal these figures by concentrating on the high command is to hide the reality.

Finally, as in any documentary about Stalin, we have an obligatory passage through the famine in Ukraine. Here they say, "Soviet power managed to murder 4 million Ukrainians in the most baffling secrecy."

In his devastating review of Anne Applebaum's book *Red Famine*, top agricultural historian Mark Tauger (West Virginia University) gives a completely different version of the story:

> Stalin and other leaders made concessions to Ukraine in terms of taxes and clearly tried to balance the subsistence needs of Ukraine and other regions, especially those of people in cities and industrial sites who could not access the alternative foods that some peasants had access to in order to survive (see, for example, Applebaum, ch. 12). The Soviet leaders did not understand the poor harvest of 1932: they thought that the peasants were withholding food in order to fix prices on the private market, as some had done in 1928. They were worried about the capture of Manchuria by the Japanese in 1931-1932 and the Nazi victory in Germany in early 1933, and feared that nationalist groups in Poland and Austria would inspire a nationalist rebellion in the Ukraine. In the face of these "threats," the Soviet leaders did not dare to make the USSR look weak by admitting famine and importing a lot of food, which they had done several times before. The famine and the insufficiency of Soviet relief can be attributed to the bad harvests, as well as to the incompetence and paranoia of the leadership in the face of foreign threats and peasant speculators: a retaliatory version of moral economy.[4]

As for the deaths caused by this famine, this is what Viktor Zemskov writes, whose statistics are used by all historians, both left and right:

> In the literature there are absurd figures of 6 to 10 million deaths, of which 3 to 7 million are in Ukraine. However, thanks to demographic statistics, we know that there were 782,000 births and 668,000 deaths in Ukraine in 1932, while there were 359,000 births and 1.3 million deaths in 1933.[5]

---

3 See Roger REESE, "The Red Army and the Great Purges," in J.A. GETTY. and R.T. MANNING, *Stalinist Terror, New Perspectives*, Cambridge, 1993, p. 199.

4 Source: https://historynewsnetwork.org/article/169438.

5 See his interview in *La Vanguardia*, https://rebelion.org/los-muertos-de-stalin/.

Drive to the East

If it were only that, we would not get out of the classic anti-communist propaganda. However, the most disturbing thing is that ARTE is also part of today's bellicose anti-Russian propaganda. This should be of concern not only to communists, but also to all citizens committed to peace or at least to those who, curious as it may seem to the dominant ideology and anti-Russian state racism that plagues our regions, are not in the mood for a Third World War.

Indeed, we were very surprised to find that, formally, this documentary does not even recognize the legitimacy of the current Russian-Polish border.

ARTE tells us: "On September 17, 1939, the Red Army invaded eastern Poland." Of course, this is false.

The Red Army recovered the lands populated by Belarusian and Ukrainian speaking people that had been confiscated from what was later the USSR by the Polish offensive during the Russo-Polish war of 1919-1921. This war cost the lives of tens of thousands of Soviet prisoners starving to death in the camps, but this does not seem to interest ARTE.

On the contrary, the documentary speaks of a division of Poland in which "Stalin intends to take his share of the cake."

In a context in which the Polish state had ceased to exist, the Soviet power tried, through the recovery of these lost territories, to push the future front with Germany as far west as possible. But of course, if the documentary presents the Barbarossa offensive as a "plot twist," there is no way to understand any of this.

ARTE explains to us that Poland has been shifted from east to west, as if to imply that it is not in its place and should be further east. With this new version of the "Drang nach Osten," i.e. the push to the East, of dismal memory, when will they stop recognizing the Oder-Neisse line?

Let us remember: it is with this revanchist Germany that Macron, under the recent Treaty of Aix-la-Chapelle, plans to share the French nation's defense and seat on the UN Security Council.

Khrushchev, Missing

Of all the documents that have been presented to attest to the official version of Katyn, the documentary chose to present the March 5, 1940 letter from Beria to Stalin, in which the NKVD chief would ask for authorization to execute the Polish prisoners.

The documentary takes the trouble to explain that this letter receives the signed approval of all Politburo members, of which two approved by telephone, with the exception of Nikita Khrushchev "who, being in the Ukraine, could not be contacted."

As if the telephone did not exist in Ukraine... Of course, ARTE will not say that a scientific analysis proved that the last page of the letter, the one bearing Beria's signature, was written on a typewriter different from the one used to write the first three pages. The analysis and the professional diplomas of the handwriting expert can be found on Sergei Stryguine's website.[6]

There are many other inconsistencies in the "secret file," such as an anachronistic seal of the CPSU on another letter (name of the Party which will not be given until 1952) or even the mention by Shelepin, director of the KGB from 1959 to 1962, and of an execution in the same camps of Starobelsk and Ostashkov, while the official version mentions that the prisoners were transferred from these camps. From here, we understand better why a forgery, which incriminates the Politburo except Khrushchev, could have been fabricated under the command of the latter. In the end, Mr. K. renounced this machination because of the difficulty of denying his co-responsibility as a member of the Politburo.

For the German report, and then for the Soviet report, the documentary presents all the witnesses as manipulated persons. However, in his book *L'Énigme du massacre de Katyn. Les preuves. La solution.* (Éditions Delga, 2019) [*The Mystery of the Katyn Massacre: The Evidence. The Solution*],[7] Grover Furr clearly shows that witnesses who had no interest in defending the Soviet thesis did not hesitate to testify in its favor in Nuremberg, such as Dr. František Hájek, who resided in the West.

6 Экспертиза машинописных шрифтов "письма Берии No. 794/Б," http://katyn.ru/index.php?go=Pages&in=view&id=946 (expert opinion on typewritings of "letter to Beria No. 794/b").

7 **Ed. Note:** First published in English by Erythos Press, 2019.

A Fanatical Nazi Presented as a Medical and Scientific Endorsement of the Documentary

Finally, let us move on to the height of astonishment: the ARTE documentary presents as a kind of scientific endorsement of the German report on the participation of the forensic doctor Orsós, from Budapest. Why do they not tell us, as Grover Furr shows us in his work, that the latter was a fanatical Nazi? On July 18, 1941, during a debate in the Hungarian Upper House on the third anti-Jewish law prohibiting marriage and sexual relations between members of the Jewish and Christian communities, Orsós had demanded that the prohibition be extended even to marriage and relations between Roma and Hungarians. Orsós wanted, furthermore, to keep Jewish doctors away from Christian patients.

Grover Furr comments:

> This criminal record did not prevent the Madden Commission from subpoenaing Nazi Orsós as a witness.
>
> Neither Cienciala, nor Sanford, nor, as far as I know, any of the other studies that highlight the "official" version account for Orsós' Nazi collaboration. This would compromise the supposed "objectivity" of the conclusions of the medical commission headed by Orsós, which was convened by the Nazis in Katyn.
>
> According to the German report, it is clear that Orsós was summoned only by an article he had published in a Hungarian medical journal in 1941. He concluded that the presence in the skull of a corpse of a hard substance which he called "pseudocallus," or decomposition of the brain matter, proved that the skull had been buried for at least three years.

The term *pseudocallus* remains a mystery to the scientific community.

For the next anti-communist documentary, will the ARTE network present Dr. Mengele's theses as scientific evidence, or will it choose Goering as a moral witness? It is true that, by adopting the official version of Katyn, ARTE simply takes up that of Joseph "the more-exorbitant-the more convincing" Goebbels.

Naturally, about Goebbels' version, the documentary also fails to mention the contradictions in the German report, such as the bullet casings presented sideways so that the year of manufacture cannot be seen, the inscriptions bearing the name of the city of Lemberg (German name for Lvov or Lviv), the mention of a "letter written in German by a prisoner to the camp director."

Worse still, the documentary hides contradictions that appear in the report, which have been known since the time of Nuremberg.

In fact, ARTE tells us that there were no traces of insects on either the bodies or the clothing, so the execution took place during the cold season of 1940 (according to the Nazi version) and not during the autumn of 1941 (according to the Soviet version).

Dr. Palmieri, an Italian member of the medical team taken to Katyn by the Nazis, had found traces of insects.

During this testimony in Nuremberg, Dr. Markov pointed out this contradiction in the German report:

> As for insects and their larvae, the statement in the general report that they had not been found is in flagrant contradiction with the conclusions of Professor Palmieri, which are recorded in his personal notes concerning the corpse which he himself dissected. In this protocol, which is published in the German white book itself, it is stated that there were traces of insect remains and their larvae in the mouths of the corpses.[8]

On Beria's "Bounties"

We also interviewed Grover Furr regarding the following claim in the ARTE documentary, which we suspected was not substantiated in any way:

> By top-secret order of October 26, 1940, Beria rewards the NKVD agents who executed the Poles with one month's supplementary salary. This order reveals the names of the murderers. In total, 40 Chekists liquidated 22,000 people in six weeks [...] In just two nights, all the families of the executed officers, i.e. 60,000 people, were arrested and sent to the gulag.

This was the response of the U.S. researcher:

> You are right, there is no evidence that these rewards were given for shooting anyone anywhere, let alone Poles in Katyn. Nikita Petrov, a researcher and senior official of the "Memorial" society, published an article in Novaya Gazeta on April 27, 2015, claiming that he had identified NKVD executioners from the "bounties" order of October 26, 1940.
>
> Following this statement, Petrov published a book in which he develops his thesis further. First in Polish, Poczet Katów Katyńskich (Warsaw, 2015), and then in Russian, *Nagrajdeny za rasstrel* ([*Awarded for execution*], Moscow, 2016). I have both of these books. Like the Novaya Gazeta article, they contain NO evidence that these men were involved in the Katyn case or that the bounties were related to Katyn. The case of the expulsion of the families seems to be a reference to the text of the "Beria letter," the most important document in the "sealed file No. 1" [of

8 *Nuremberg Trials*, Volume XVII, p. 354. *Cf.* Furr's book, p. 94.

which all evidence points to, as we have discussed, a forgery—A. M.]. I can find no other reference to it.

To Conclude

The ARTE documentary concludes with images of the disinterment of bodies while the voice-over talks about the Piatykhatky and Mednoe sites, the two other Katyn-related massacre sites revealed by the Soviet "secret dossier."

The images from ARTE, in black and white, likely date back to the war, while the supposed execution sites, besides the Katyn site, were only revealed during the time of Gorbachev. Why talk about these two sites with images that have nothing to do with it? Well, simply because the bodies of the Polish prisoners were not found at Pyatykhatky or Mednoe.

On the contrary, two badges of Polish policemen were found, supposedly buried in Mednoe, 1,200 km from there, in Volodymyr-Volynskyi, western Ukraine, and in SS mass graves dating back to 1941. As Grover Furr demonstrated in 2013, this discovery collapses the official version and explains why excavations in Ukraine ceased without any DNA expertise or subsequent identification being attempted.

Of course, we are sure that these approximations and oversights of the documentary will be corrected in the next version...

In the meantime, we can only urge the reader concerned with accuracy to turn to recent and well-supported studies on the issue, *L'énigme du massacre de Katyn. Les preuves. La solution* [*The Mystery of the Katyn massacre. The evidence. The solution*] (*nota bene*: not to be confused with the previous edition, by the same author and with the same publisher Delga, of the work: *Le massacre de Katyn. Une réfutation de la version "officielle"?* [*The "Official" Version of the Katyn Massacre Disproven?*] which dates from 2015 and which, of a more modest dimension, focuses mainly on the question of the excavations in Volodymyr-Volynskyi).[9]

Grover Furr, in his 2019 book, has studied all the evidence that cannot have been forged or fabricated by the Germans or the Soviets. On the basis of an exhaustive study of this "irrefutable evidence," Furr

9 **Ed. Note:** For Furr's "Mystery" book, see note on page 12 above. The previous Furr work was originally published in *Socialism and Democracy*, Vol. 27, No. 2,pp. 96-129 [copyright Taylor & Francis], accessible at https://www.tandfonline.com/doi/full/10.1080/08854300.2013.795268.

concludes that there is *no* evidence of Soviet guilt. All the evidence from indisputably authentic primary sources indicates either German guilt or Soviet non-guilt. The *only* way to accuse the Soviets is to "believe" the documents in "sealed dossier No. 1" handed over by the Russian government to the Poles. However, they have been reliably qualified as forgeries. The German report of 1943 is also full of contradictions.

Historians do not have to "believe" the sources. The thesis of Soviet guilt in Katyn cannot be sustained if one leaves aside the doubtful evidence, and if one studies only the evidence called into question by the UN, what Furr calls the "irreproachable" evidence.

March 1, 2020

What the Film *Mr. Jones* and its Peculiar Protagonist Keeps Quiet

Occasionally filmed with a shoulder-mounted camera to claim authenticity, Agnieszka Holland's film "Mr. Jones," released in 2019, barely manages to conceal its commissioned nature. Financed by the Ukrainian state and various Polish institutions, "Mr. Jones" could, given its serious political implications, have been the subject of commentary other than aesthetic-cinematic, at a time when the press presents itself as bent on unmasking so-called "fake news."

Titled in Ukrainian "The Price of Truth" (Ціна правди), in Polish "Citizen Jones" (*Obywatel Jones*), and, more simply, "Mr. Jones" in English, the film is set entirely from the point of view of the Welsh journalist who investigated the famine in Ukraine in March 1933. However, much to the chagrin of its generous contributors, this film that purports to be a tribute to the truth and its brave defenders has already been the subject of a full-blown takedown by... none other than the family of the main protagonist.

Family, I Hate You

Naturally, we cannot count on the French press to convey this reprobation. However, the article did not come from a marginal source, since it was published in the columns of the *Sunday Times*, the supplement of the famous newspaper, and was signed by the grandnephew of the Welsh journalist.[1] He drew on the important work done by his mother, Dr. Margaret Siriol Colley, who in her lifetime had helped to assemble the archives of Gareth Jones (i.e. his uncle)[2] and published his biography: *More than a Grain of Truth; The Official Biography of Gareth Jones*.[3]

In fact, these various works had been the subject of all the attention of the Ukrainian government, which has since made the almost unknown journalist a hero of Ukraine. Despite these honors, the family is not at all happy with how their ancestor is portrayed and, in opposition to what the film relates, his great-nephew says:

> [Gareth Jones] didn't witness any dead bodies or any cannibalism, let alone take part in any; he never saw any grain requisition, forced labor or body-carts; he was never chased, never ran, never hid or disguised himself on his hike along the railway line. He was never imprisoned. Far from the claims of the film I don't think he ever felt himself to be in any great danger, protected by his fluency in Russian, his charm and a useful VIP gratis visa. Furthermore, the narrative frame of the film, that Gareth met George Orwell, is simply not true, despite James Norton and the filmmakers attempts to spin otherwise. Similarly, for the claim that Gareth inspired *Animal Farm* there is no firm evidence.

To which he adds:

> [...] the internet is littered with untruths as a result of this film: that Gareth was "a Welsh diplomat who worked for Chamberlain and once interviewed Hitler" (he was not and did not); that he met George Orwell (he did not); that he went to Russia to interview Stalin (he did not); that he WAS murdered by the Soviets (there is no conclusive evidence for that). The filmmakers have admitted that Gareth did

1 **Ed. Note:** Published in the *Sunday Times* on 26th January 2020, "Mr. Jones: The True Story not Seen on Film," Phillip Colley. An edited and non-paywalled version is available here: https://www.garethjones.org/mr_jones/true_story.htm.

2 See: https://www.garethjones.org/.

3 **Ed. Note:** Published in the UK by Lume Books, 2020.

> not witness all the events depicted in their film but told me they feel justified in using him to portray their version of what happened in the Holodomor. [The latter being the name given to the genocidal famine thesis in Ukrainian—A. M.].

This is a bit messy, isn't it?

Citizen Ukraine

As for William Randolph Hearst, the newspaper magnate who inspired *Citizen Kane* and who published three articles by Jones on the USSR in 1935,[4] he is presented in the film as a passive actor in the affair, secluded in his mansion and who had not agreed to publish Jones until after he had been harassed, and finally convinced, by the young man's persuasive force. In reality, the "six million dead" campaign, which was spread in the Hearst press, had many other causes and spokesmen, in particular the pseudonymous Thomas Walker who had not hesitated to illustrate the famine with photos dating from 1921.[5]

Even the website dedicated to Gareth Jones, and which supports the "genocidal" famine thesis, does not shy from this:

> A fake correspondent, Thomas Walker, who turned out to be a fugitive detainee whose "real" name was Robert Green, had prompted Hearst to publish a series of five articles recounting his purported foray into the Ukraine in 1934, where he was even able to take pictures of the famine "in progress." Louis Fischer of The Nation revealed that these articles turned out to be complete frauds, thanks to his being informed by Soviet authorities of Walker's exact dates of entry into and departure from the USSR (which "proved" Walker did not have time to travel to Ukraine).

It is also acknowledged that "Louis Fischer successfully exposed Thomas Walker's articles and photos to be a fraud."[6]

However, the website ventures the following hypothesis :

> Though Thomas Walker / Robert Green was held up to be a pawn of Hearst, below I would like to put forward the hypothesis that he was more likely to have been a Soviet patsy, in their very successful propaganda of hiding the truth of a famine in Ukraine at any time in the 1930s, as Gareth's truthful observations were tarnished

---

4 See: https://www.garethjones.org/soviet_articles/soviet_articles.htm.

5 See Douglas Tottle, *Fraud, Famine, and Fascism: the Ukrainian Genocide Myth from Hitler to Harvard,* Progress Books, Toronto, 1987. Available online at: http://www.rationalrevolution.net/special/library/tottlefraud.pdf.

6 See: https://www.garethjones.org/soviet_articles/thomas_walker/thomas_walker.htm.

by the same brush.[7]

We understand better why the Ukrainian nationalists were interested in this forgotten journalist Gareth Jones. Indeed, when the evidence of the fraudulent procedures used to accuse the Soviet Union through the Hearst press could no longer be denied, Jones' supporters were nevertheless convinced that the latter's testimony was completely authentic and sincere and that Hearst had simply been abused by the criminal Walker.

This is rather doubtful when it is known that during the Spanish-American War (1898), Hearst was already publishing false images of Spanish soldiers locking up Cubans in concentration camps where the latter were supposed to die of starvation or disease. After the war, he boasted of having invested more than a million dollars to better unleash hostilities. Inventor of the so-called "yellow press," Hearst did not hide his sympathy for the Nazi regime either. The website on Gareth Jones even acknowledges that an agreement between Goebbels and Hearst had been reached as early as June 1934 to relay Nazi propaganda, but that it actually occurred just after Jones' visit to Hearst: *phew*, honor is saved... Hearst's hostility towards Roosevelt's New Deal may have also played a role in this matter.

In this connection, Gareth Jones is presented as having interviewed Hitler and Goebbels for purely journalistic reasons. He was one of the first foreign journalists to travel on Hitler's private plane in late February 1933. However, after his expulsion from Russia, what the film does not tell is that "Mr. Jones" returned to Berlin on March 29, 1933 to publish his communiqué on the horrors seen in the Soviet Union.[8] Approximately one month after the repression decreed after the Reichstag fire and while the repression was being carried out against communists and other opponents, there is no doubt that Gareth Jones found attentive readers in the German capital. In short, he made the report in the USSR in March 1933 between a report on Hitler at the end of February 1933 and a communiqué in Berlin on March 29.

The Good and the Bad?

The journalistic probity of Gareth Jones is highlighted in the film by the principle of a counter-model, in this case Walter Duranty, who was

7 *Ibid.*

8 See: https://www.garethjones.org/soviet_articles/walking_tour.htm.

the New York Times correspondent in Moscow from 1922 to 1938 and winner of the Pulitzer Prize in 1932. The bête noire of the Ukrainian nationalists who have long sought to withdraw his award, and who also appears on the list sent by George Orwell in 1949 to the Information Research Department,[9] Duranty is portrayed without surprise in Mr. Jones as a most vile, depraved and corrupt being, who uses his reputation as a great award-winning journalist to cover up Soviet power.

Yet, when one rereads his article dated March 31, 1933, intended to respond to Gareth Jones's statement published two days earlier in Berlin, Duranty appears mainly focused on refuting Jones regarding what constituted the essential question of the time and would remain so, namely the USSR's ability to resist a Nazi or Western attack.[10] While Gareth Jones describes the USSR as "on the verge of a terrific smash," Duranty notes that these terms remind him word for word of the propaganda used in the Anglo-Saxon press during the Civil War. In this case, as for the resilience and resistance of the USSR, it is clear that the facts corroborated what Duranty said and disproved Gareth Jones' assertions. It will take, then, more elements for the Ukrainian nationalists to make Duranty withdraw an award obtained in 1932 for his coverage of the Soviet reality in 1931, which dealt insufficiently to their liking with events that should have taken place at least a year later... It is true that the inquisitorial procedures resemble, by their absurd grandiloquence, and that we are not far from what happened to Bishop Priscillian in Buñuel's *The Milky Way*: the exhumation of his remains after his heresy had been recognized.[11]

As for the famine itself, Duranty's article in response to Jones is

9 **Ed. Note:** A secret British Cold War anti-communist and pro-colonial propaganda department that officially operated from 1948-77, created by the Atlee Labour administration. George Orwell submitted a list of 38 people, ostensibly to indicate who would be unsuitable for working for the propaganda department, including Walter Duranty. However, it is essentially a way for Orwell to highlight suspected communists and "fellow travellers." Orwell also provided commentary, labelling actor and activist Paul Robeson as "very anti-white" and highlighting those who he thought had a "tendency towards homosexuality" (at a time shortly after the British government had insisted on chemical castration for "war hero" Alan Turing for his homosexuality). It should also be noted that Animal Farm was translated and distributed around the word as a tool of propaganda by the IRD.

10 Reproduced on the website dedicated to Gareth Jones: https://www.garethjones.org/margaret_siriol_colley/The%20exhibition/rebuttal_duranty.htm.

11 Although he was indeed beheaded for heresy, Priscillian, nevertheless, would not have undergone this punishment after his death.

neither caricatured nor exaggerated, since it actually recognizes "an endemic mortality due to diseases caused by malnutrition." Moreover, he does not hesitate to partly agree with Gareth Jones about the reality of the catastrophe:

> Returning to Mr. Jones. He told me that there was practically no bread in the villages he had visited and that the adults were dazed, skinny and despondent, but that he had not seen any dead or dying animals or human beings. I believed this because I knew it was accurate not only in parts of the Ukraine, but also in parts of the North Caucasus and lower Volga and, moreover, in Kazakhstan, where the attempt to transform the nomadic herdsmen of the period of Abraham and Isaac into collective grain producers in 1933 yielded very deplorable results.

In fact, Jones did not claim to have seen corpses. The Berlin communiqué rather relates indirect testimonies, which were taken up in the film:

> I walked alone through villages and twelve collective farms. Everywhere there was a cry, "There is no bread, we are dying." This cry came to me from all regions of Russia. On a train, a communist told me that there was no famine. I threw the crust of a piece of bread I had taken from my own stash into the spittoon. My traveling companion, who was a peasant, took it out and ate it greedily. I poured orange peels into the spittoon. Again, the peasant took them out and devoured them. The communist calmed down. A foreign expert who returned from Kazakhstan told me that one in five million people died of starvation. I can believe it.

The same is true in his article published two days later in the *Evening Standard*[12] or even in his articles published by Hearst.[13] In his reply to Duranty's rejoinder, Jones said, "says that I saw in the villages no dead human beings nor animals. That is true, but one does not need a particularly nimble brain to grasp that even in the Russian famine districts the dead are buried and that there the dead animals are devoured."[14] On the other hand, it is worth remembering that Jones explains: "my evidence was based upon letters written by German colonists in Russia, appealing for help to their compatriots in Germany." Definitely, Germany always appears in the background... yet in any case, as we have already seen, Duranty, Jones himself, and even the latter's great-nephew all agree that Jones did not witness corpses littering the roads, nor carts carrying corpses, nor did he engage in cannibalism during his journey in

12 See: https://www.garethjones.org/soviet_articles/famine_rules_russia.htm.

13 In the *New York American*, *Los Angeles Examiner*, and the *Sunday American*, January 12-14, 1935.

14 See: https://www.garethjones.org/soviet_articles/jones_replies.htm.

the Kharkov region, contrary to what the film portrays. Under these circumstances, and as far as I know, no one in the communist camp today intends to deny anyone's suffering or absolve the Soviet leadership of serious mistakes it may have committed. The only remaining means to clarify this matter are the methods of historical research.

Back to Square One

We return, then, to the starting point of the university debate. In this field, Hollywood-style cinema will find it difficult to refute Mark Tauger, the best university specialist on the subject, who is also a specialist in the history of agriculture and of this region of the world. We can also cite historians Wheatcroft, Davies and others.[15]

The causes of the invalidation of the genocidal character of the famine as determined by Tauger have been the subject of several university articles in English and a French translation,[16] but can be summarized for the hurried reader by referring to the extended Tauger quote on page 19.

Evidently, these elements of context do not appear at all in "Mr. Jones." By way of explanation, in addition to the voluntary nature of the famine ("man-made famine," the term comes from an article by Jones in the Hearst press), the film seeks to corroborate the nationalist thesis of a punishment inflicted by Stalin on the Ukrainian people. And this, despite creating an obvious internal contradiction, since Gareth Jones himself spoke in his article of famine outside Ukraine ("of all the regions of Russia, of the Volga, of Siberia, of White Russia, of the North Caucasus and Central Asia").[17] As expected, in "Mr. Jones" all the victims speak Ukrainian, and the executioners speak Russian. For the Western viewer it doesn't matter, all this is merged into the subtitles. So it goes: what is understood *in the text* as a Russophobic nationalist delirium in a country where Russian is now banned and where communists are forbidden, if not simply burned alive,[18] can be presented under the label of

15 Robert W. Davies and Stephen G. Wheatcroft, *The Years of Hunger: Soviet Agriculture, 1931-1933*, Palgrave Macmillan, New York, 2004.

16 See his book, in its French version, *Famine et transformation agricole en USSR* [Famine and agricultural transformation in the USSR], Éditions Delga, Paris, 2017.

17 Berlin communiqué of March 29, 1933 reported in several media, among others: *The Manchester Guardian* and the *New York Evening Post*.

18 As in the fire at the house of trade unions in Odessa in 2014.

"anti-totalitarian film" in the West.

Finally, after the preparation of the artillery of complacent historians, none of whom—let us remember—has Mark Tauger's competence and legitimacy on the subject, plus the full-blown bombardment of Hollywood-style propaganda reviewed by Polish and Ukrainian nationalists, there is nothing left but to send in the trench cleaners of the fake left. Likewise, the so-called New Anti-Capitalist Party (NPA) in France was quick to talk about the "undeniable qualities" of the film.[19] How could they not?

July 12, 2020

19 See: https://npa2009.org/actualite/culture/lombre-de-staline.

When Famine Feeds the West

Post scriptum:
What They Don't Tell Us About *Mr. Jones*

My heartfelt thanks to Annie Lacroix-Riz.

The Famine of 1921 to the Present Day

Let us return, then, not to what this film shows, but to what it seeks to conceal. Clearly, putting Gareth Jones under the spotlight has the function of silencing the fraud of the other Hearst press purveyors of Ukrainian reporting, such as Thomas Walker, who, as pointed out above, used in the *Chicago American* photographs dating from 1921 to illustrate events happening twelve years later.

Now, to give more weight to the eponymous journalist's testimony, "Mr. Jones" presents him as having seen corpses in the streets, carts full of bodies, having indulged in cannibalism, etc., while he never said anything of the sort nor produced a single photo.

Recall that, in 2006, then Ukrainian President Yushchenko also organized a photo exhibition in Sevastopol on the 1933 famine with images likewise dating back to 1921.[1] This reheating of the Hearst press propaganda was not convincing and they had to close the exhibition. The Ukrainian secret services (SBU) had to admit their mistake three years

1 See: https://lenta.ru/features/rosukr/golodomor/.

later, pointing out that "in the Soviet era, all photographs of Ukraine from 1932-1933 were destroyed and that now can be found with great difficulty and only in private archives."[2]

One might believe that these procedures are worthy exclusively of the country where the shaven skulls of Right Sektor, Svoboda et al. patrol.[3] No way! In France, for example, Nicolas Werth visibly feels no discomfort in making us swallow these almost century-old lies.[4]

Indeed, contacted by *Arrêt sur image* [*Freeze Frame*] in 2014, following the controversies surrounding the photos and reports published in the *Chicago American*, the historian replied, "These are indeed photos of the famine of 1933, he asserts, to the best of his memory (but without truly proving it) [comments are from the editorial team]."[5]

In the same report, the USSR historian Jean-Jacques Marie, more cautious, declared: "I do not know of any photo that has been published of this famine." However, he dared to explain: "In 1932-1933, no photographer could set foot in the region affected by the famine, blocked by the army and special troops."

Apparently, Jean-Jacques Marie had been defending this argument for a long time because, in a letter dated December 8, 2007, and which she kindly shared with us, Annie Lacroix-Riz had responded to him:

> Would there then be a historical example of an official ban on photography having prevented the clandestine taking of photographs? Are we lacking in clandestine photographs of "the destruction of the Jews of Europe"? Despite what we may think, the USSR was plagued, especially in the Ukraine, by various agents, mainly Germans and Poles, very often disguised as clergymen and military intelligence officers (I refer you in this regard to my explicit and documented work *Le Vatican, l'Europe et le Reich* [*The Vatican, Europe and the Reich*]). The early 1930s is when they reached their peak in this unfortunate country. They accumulated plans of military installations (I relate such an episode in *Le Vatican…* [*The Vatican…*]) but wouldn't they have taken pictures? This is a thesis absolutely inadmissible. And, since there are no photos of "1932-1933," does it seem natural to replace them with those of the 1920-1921 famine?

---

2 See: https://regnum.ru/news/polit/1138393.html.

3 **Ed. Note:** Right Sector and Svoboda are ultra-nationalist organizations currently active in Ukraine at the time of printing.

4 **Ed. Note:** Nicholas Werth (born 1950) is a French historian.

5 https://www.arretsurimages.net/articles/staline-a-t-il-deliberement-affame-lukraine.

In a recent letter (dated July 17, 2020), Ms. Lacroix-Riz also discloses the following:

> Otto Schiller, officially "agricultural attaché to the German embassy," in fact, in charge of preparations for the invasion of Ukraine, spent his time, during his tour of the USSR between spring and summer 1933 from the North Caucasus to Ukraine, photographing the villages (activity attested by the published Foreign Office holdings "on Ukraine and the Great Famine of 1932-1933," The Foreign Office and the Famine. British documents on Ukraine and the Great Famine of 1932-1933).[6] If there had been photos of corpses in 1933, they would have been released to the "Western" public.

An Exponential Famine?

Discussions regarding the reinterpretation of certain historical events, which are inevitable and even common within the context of research, are now the subject of the threat of inquisitorial lawsuits for denialism. In a very revealing text from 2008 that is still available on her website, Mrs. Lacroix-Riz, however, had an easy time demonstrating the manifest absurdity of asserting the possibility of exterminating as many people in the territory of only Eastern Ukraine as the number of Jews exterminated by the Nazi genocide over a territory ranging from France to the Urals, and all this without any photos emerging.[7]

Moreover, as the historian recalled during Arrêt sur image's investigation, the census was not conducted for twelve years, leaving a much too wide margin of interpretation. Slowdown in population growth in Ukraine between these two dates (29,043,000 people on January 1, 1927 and 30,946,000 on January 1, 1939) can be explained by many factors other than a mortality in the millions in the years 1932 and 1933, starting with the strong internal emigration to the USSR linked to collectivization.

Recently, the Russian historian Viktor Zemskov was praised by Nicolas Werth himself, albeit belatedly, for his article "On the extent of political repressions in the USSR,"[8] dated 1995 but published in an updated version in 2012, in which he arrived at the following result:

> According to our estimates, about 3 million people were victims of the famine of

6 See footnote 1 of the link: https://www.historiographie.info/ukr33maj2008.pdf

7 *Ibid.*

8 See: https://www.politpros.com/journal/read/?ID=783

1932-1933, about half of them in Ukraine. Our conclusion, of course, is not original, since historians V. P. Danilov (USSR), S. Wheatcroft (Australia) and others gave approximately the same estimates in the 80s of the 20th century. Cf. V. P. Danilov, Коллективизация: как это было, Страницы историии советского общества: факты, проблемы, люди, Moscow, 1989, p. 250.

It is interesting to note that Zemskov, although he was the historian who devoted himself to giving accurate and unbiased figures after the opening of the archives, does not feel the need to correct the view of this event that one might have had in 1989, that is, before the fall of the USSR, much less to participate in the current exaggeration concerning this issue.

In any case, it is necessary to repeat that the figures are missing and that historians are forced to extrapolate between two census periods. By way of comparison, we could draw the same arbitrary conclusions with the United States, where demographic statistics show that between 1930 and 1940, about 7 million people are observed to be "missing." Any population curve in the United States shows a line that breaks in the mid-thirties, and resumes its course thereafter. A Russian researcher, Boris Borisov, used in this regard the term of "American Holodomor"[9] linked to the Great Depression, an appellation that should of course be taken with a grain of salt, but whose reality is nothing short of terrifying.

The fact is that, unlike in the USSR, the figures for emigration to the United States are perfectly well known. Of the 10,447,000 "missing" people, only 3,054,000 can be explained by the change in migration dynamics, which shows that the years following the 1929 crisis were indeed dreadful in that country.

These emigration figures, calculated on a national scale, are difficult to dispute. However, we obviously have much less information regarding interregional migrations in the USSR, especially in the context of a massive rural exodus linked to the urbanization-industrialization of Ukraine within the framework of the second five-year plan. This will also be evident for Kazakhstan in the text provided by Mrs. Lacroix-Riz below, where we see that a thesis, prefaced by Nicolas Werth, may appear with all the customary congratulations while leaving a real artistic blur between the explanation through death and that through exodus.

9 https://www.northstarcompass.org/nsc0903/amholomor.htm

Conclusion

As we have explained in a previous article about what may constitute a statistical sample, namely the deaths recorded per year on the Baltic-White Sea Canal construction site (see page 4 of this book), 1932 and 1933 can be safely described as *anni horribiles*, since in addition to the catastrophic agricultural conditions there was also a typhus epidemic.

The famine of 1932-1933 is presented to us in the Western media as the famine par excellence, the one that should erase all the others in our heads and especially all those that occurred in the past under the capitalist regimes and those suffered in the present during the reign of the so-called "end of history." However, there are no photographs on the subject, or almost none, unlike the famine of 1921. Of course, we must admit that the NKVD would have endeavored to conceal the magnitude of the catastrophe, if only for reasons of internal security. However, such a policy would have been more or less countered by the widespread desire in the West to reveal "Stalin's crimes." So, to explain this anomaly of the absence of photographs, why would one have to dismiss out of hand, under the pretext of gratuitous, secular, and compulsory anti-Stalinism, the hypothesis that the famine of 1933 was simply smaller than that of 1921? At least, one could be prudent instead of repeating year after year those macabre exponential balances reminiscent of Cold War propaganda such as *Mein Kampf*.

Of course, it is understood that there is a clear political interest of the anti-communist propagandists to inflate, every year a little more, the figures of the "Holodomor," to vilify the man they hate the most, namely Joseph Stalin. This famine is clearly "the one they prefer" to borrow Brassens' song,[10] because the Western powers are not responsible for it, unlike those that ravaged their colonies at the same time or those in-

10 **Ed. Note:** Georges Brassens (1921-1981) was a French singer-songwriter and poet. The lyrics referenced here are from "La guerre de 14-18," a song where Brassens ironically expresses his preference for the First World War over other wars throughout history. The opening stanza captures the tone of the song (editor's translation):

Since the man writes history
Since he battles with joy at heart
Among a thousand notorious wars
If I had to make a choice
Contrary to old Homer
I would declare right away:
"Me, my colonel, the one I prefer,
It's the war of fourteen-eighteen!"

flicted on the country of the Soviets during the war improperly called "civil." It is true that it is no easy task to prove that the famine of 1932-1933 was a genocidal famine and, *a fortiori*, to paint it as a procedure intended to punish only Ukraine. However, this initiative will always leave traces, as if to lay the blame on the newly implemented collectivization. Nobody wonders why collectivization, which is supposed to have produced a famine, was precisely the phenomenon from which the USSR led by Stalin definitively overcame the infernal and pluricentennial cycle of famines affecting Russia (with the exception of the immediate post-war period), and this to take the country "from the plow to Sputnik," according to the already consecrated expression.

July 17, 2020

And in Kazakhstan?

Annie Lacroix-Riz[1]

Isabelle Ohayon has very well grasped the insurmountable contradiction associated with the "emptying" of many villages in her thesis *La sédentarisation des Kazakhs dans l'URSS de Staline. Collectivisation et changement social (1928-1945)* [*The Sedentarization of Kazakhs in Stalin's USSR: Collectivization and Social Change (1928-1945)*].[2] With her original archive severely lacking in content, the author is forced to re employ the usual simple assumptions, which she, by the way, immediately disproves. Naturally, under the guidance of Nicolas Werth, Ms. Ohayon had to adhere to the thesis of the millions of deaths in Kazakhstan. Chapter 7, "Migrating to Survive, Fleeing Famine and Epidemics (1931-1933)," announces the study of "a tentacular famine" (p. 227*ff.*). Without providing more than generalities and estimates in this respect, in the absence of sources, the work is full of references of this type:

> On the demographic level, the mortality data available—incomplete because of under-recording, scattered, local or too general, produced on the dates of the catastrophe—do not allow us to propose a precise overall estimate of the human losses due to the famine. The problem is even more complex considering that the population deficit is also explained by the negative migratory balance experienced by Kazakhstan between 1930 and 1934. It is therefore necessary to try to distinguish between displacements and deaths. In any case, it remains very difficult to follow the evolution of the famine and the consequent mortality year after year,

1 To broaden the discussion beyond Ukraine in the period of 1932-1933, we quote (with her permission) what Mrs. Lacroix-Riz sends us regarding the same situation, but this time in Kazakhstan, concerning Isabelle Ohayon's thesis, prefaced by Nicolas Werth.

2 Paris, Maisonneuve et Larose, 2005 [**Ed. Note:** At time of writing, this does not appear to have been translated to English.]

> although it is possible to define approximately a periodization of its extension and its decline" (p. 228).

In short, as the author repeatedly admits, a displaced peasant is not necessarily a "famine" casualty. By way of summary, below the conclusions of chapters 8 and 9 are presented.

Concluding chapter 8, on p. 326:

> Sedentarization as it had occurred as a consequence of the trauma of the exodus and the death of a third of the population, in sectors of activity alien to the Kazakhs, was pushed as a last resort, causing an inevitable and brutal acculturation.

Exodus and death, but in what proportion? The reader will never know. And the conclusion of chapter 9, on p. 352:

> [...] it can be affirmed, despite the lack of data, that the sedentarization and Sovietization of the Kazakhs led to a certain deterioration of the genealogical memory, without destroying the clan as a criterion of identity belonging.

Therefore, not the least aspect of the enormous deception, contemporary Kazakhstan would have lost all memory of this massacre. The same phenomenon occurs in Soviet Ukraine, where no one has ever remembered massive deaths due to famine in 1933 (the "testimony" came only from the then Polish Ukraine, a phenomenon that led consecutively to the German, Vatican, Polish, etc. campaign which started in the summer of 1933, after the excellent harvest of July).[3] This does not prevent the author from giving an astonishing general conclusion in chapter 7, "The experience of collectivization and sedentarization led to the death of about one third of the Kazakh population (between 1.15 and 1.4 million people, according to estimates) and the final emigration of 500,000 people" (p. 363). And a few lines later the following observation: "The success of the proletarianization of the Kazakhs is illustrated by the progress of their share in industry, which rose from 20% to 45% of the workforce between 1928 and 1936" (pp. 362-363). And repeated on p. 365:

> However, the losses suffered by Kazakhstan are unparalleled in proportional terms in the USSR during this period, accounting for more than 30% of the population, and to the deaths must be added the final emigration of half a million Kazakhs.

In his enthusiasm for the thesis of the candidate from the early 2000s, based on a problematic obtained by sheer force, the obligation to propagate the Doxa under the threat of career ruin, Nicolas Werth has lost a sense of the ridiculous. I quote his laudatory preface, pp. 9-11,

3 See note 1 of the link: https://www.historiographie.info/ukr33maj2008.pdf.

to this "capital book, on a profoundly unknown subject and of crucial importance for the understanding of Stalinism."

> The "modernization" initiative which was to lead to the Sovietization of the traditional Kazakh society and to move the Kazakhs from a "natural economy" to a "socialist economy" resulted, between 1931 and 1933, in an unprecedented demographic catastrophe: one third of the Kazakh population disappeared, a proportion without equivalent in any other part of the world, not even in the other regions of the USSR hit by the shortages and famines following the forced collectivization of the countryside. Between one million one hundred thousand and one million four hundred thousand Kazakhs died as a result of famine and epidemics—which represents, in absolute figures, the number of dead in France during the Great War—while six hundred thousand Kazakhs fled their country for good" (p. 9).

This is contradicted by the whole of this same thesis, which does not precisely choose between "the exodus and the death of a third of the population."

Nicolas Werth then glosses, according to tradition, on the "taboo" that would have buried forever the dreadful memory of such an ordeal:

> A remarkable fact, observed by Isabelle Ohayon in the course of her research in the field, is that the Kazakhs themselves, with the exception of a few historians, have remained surprisingly silent to this day about this terrible violence imposed on their society in the first half of the 1930s.

Consecutive silence:

> What are the reasons for this silence? Undoubtedly having carried out, after that, a successful acculturation.

Is that so? In French families, people still spoke until recently of the dead of the First World War, 10.5% of the male working population, but in Kazakhstan (as in interwar Soviet Ukraine), even the memory of the torrents of the dead would have been forgotten. First, the secessionist Ukrainians gave the figure of 6 million, to match the number of Jews massacred by the Third Reich, before proposing much higher figures, 7, 9, 10, 12, up to 17 million to my knowledge, for a total population of around thirty million Soviet Ukrainians. They were really skilled in manipulation through propaganda, these Soviets. We wonder then why the Americans defeated them in 1989.

July 2022

For a Few Canards More

Some Other Common Claims Regarding the USSR

On the Fate of Soviet Prisoners After the War

A statement, among other enormities, from the unspeakable *Apocalypse: Stalin*,[1] but one that we have been hearing for a long time:

> The fate of these Soviet prisoners will be tragic. The survivors will be deported by Stalin because they surrendered to the enemy.

Data extracted from the archives by Viktor Zemskov (GARF. F. 9526. *Op*. 4a. D. 1. L. 62, 223-226) shatter the myth of the alleged almost universal repression of Soviet servicemen who were in fascist captivity. Indeed, of the 1,539,475 prisoners of war who returned to the USSR between October 1944 and March 1, 1946 from Germany and other countries, more than 280,000 were demobilized from the army and consequently returned home. The bulk of the POWs, of serviceable age, were reintegrated into the army. Regarding the special contingent handed over to the NKVD (which represented less than 15%, i.e. 226,157 persons), Zemskov adds that "it should not be forgotten that most of this category of repatriated POWs had joined the enemy's military or police services at some point after their capture."

1 **Ed. Note:** See page vii.

The USSR Won the War Thanks to the US?

According to historian Geoffrey Roberts, the aid given to the Soviet war army between 1941 and 1945 amounted to 10% of the total. Roberts also specifies this important fact: "Most of this aid arrived after Stalingrad, so its main role was to facilitate victory rather than stave off defeat" (*Les Guerres de Staline* [*Stalin's Wars*], Delga, 2014, p. 215).[2]

The historian also mentions "the abrupt manner in which the Americans cut off expeditions of material on loan and lease to the Soviet Union from the moment the Germans surrendered" (*Ibid*., p. 355).

On the Soviet economy during the war and the role played by Lend-Lease aid, Roberts' primary source was the work of Mark Harrison, in particular:

1. *Soviet Planning in Peace and War 1938-1945*, Cambridge, Cambridge University Press, Cambridge, 1985;
2. *The Economics of World War II: Six Great Powers in International Comparison*, Cambridge University Press, Cambridge, 1998;
3. *Accounting for War: Soviet Production, Employment, and the Defence Burden, 1940-1945*, Cambridge University Press, Cambridge, 1996.

Did Stalin let the Nazis raze Warsaw when he had a chance to liberate it? Roberts states that:

> This [above shown] picture of consistent, if ill-fated, Soviet efforts to capture Warsaw in summer 1944 runs completely counter to an alternative scenario: that when the Red Army reached the Vistula it deliberately halted its offensive operations to allow the Germans time to crush a popular uprising in the city. (Ibid., p. 266 *ff*.).[3]

Lysenko: Charlatan and Impostor?

This is a Manichean and caricatured vision that does not correspond to the real movement of the history of science.

First of all, Trofim Lysenko could not have aspired to the role he played without his early successes, in particular the formation of spring wheat variety from winter wheat by vernalization.

2 **Ed. Note:** English Edition printed by Yale University Press, 2008. The quote above is found on p. 164.

3 **Ed. Note:** This quote and surrounding context found on p. 206 of the English edition.

Moreover, the historian of biology Guillaume Suing, who is dedicated among other things to "overcoming the black legend of Lysenko,"[4] and to recalling the history of what he calls "real ecology"[5] in socialist countries, shows that, whatever his personal shortcomings and despite the erroneous ideology of the "two sciences" linked to his person, Lysenko could today be attributed a role resembling that of a precursor of "sustainable" agriculture:

> "Lysenkoist" agronomists were abundantly caricatured by post-war Westerners simply because they opposed the miraculous so-called system of intensive agriculture (chemical fertilizers and pesticides). While this allowed maximum profit in a minimum of time, today it is clear that it has contributed to the massive destruction of soils on a global scale, and has been the source of innumerable and undeniable long-term ecological catastrophes. But this, of course, is not a "hoax."
>
> Lysenko and his collaborators wished, even if the results were not immediate, to develop sustainable agriculture throughout the territory based on techniques that are now fully accepted: "planting under vegetation cover," "agroforestry-pastoral balance" linked to crop rotation and the development of "forest strips" between cultivated fields, [...] in general, they preferred soil fertilization by biological means rather than by chemical means [...] within the framework of extensive agriculture (and not intensive in the capitalist sense of the term).[6]

Even with regard to the famous "inheritance of characters acquired by habit," with which Lysenko opposed classical genetics that has inheritance pass through random mutations selected secondarily by the environment, Suing points out that it is today's biologists who are again putting this idea on the agenda under the euphemistic title of "epigenetics." To which he adds:

> Is it not indeed more than urgent, when searching for an alternative to increasingly incriminated pesticides, to recognize the ability of a plant to transmit hereditarily, over several generations, acquired resistance to specific stress or certain parasites?
>
> The irony of history is that it is the Western geneticists themselves, once vilified by the "proletarian agronomist," who are launching this profound revolution in biology, overturning all the mechanistic dogmas of formal genetics as well as those

---

4 Guillaume Suing, *Évolution: la preuve par Marx. Dépasser la légende noire de Lyssenko* [*Evolution: the proof by Marx. Overcoming the black legend of Lysenko*], Delga, Paris, 2016, preface by Georges Gastaud.

5 Id, *L'écologie réelle: une histoire soviétique et cubaine* [*Real Ecology: A Soviet and Cuban history*], Delga, Paris, 2018, preface by Viktor Dedaj. [**Ed. Note:** Iskra Books aims to translate and publish *L'écologie réelle* [*Real Ecology*] in the near future.]

6 Guillaume Suing, "*Lyssenko, un imposteur?*" [Lysenko, an imposter?], *Investig'action*, May 10, 2016.

> of capitalist agronomy. They seek to find an alternative to an intensive agriculture that was truly dangerous and deadly, both for nature and humanity.[7]

Did Stalin Deliver German Communists to Hitler?

Former Communist Margarete Buber-Neumann, who testified at Kravchenko's trial and joined Koestler after the war, accused the Soviet regime of having handed over German anti-fascists, including herself, to the Third Reich during the period of the Non-Aggression Pact.[8]

Nothing in the Soviet archives came to confirm the existence of what she called a "welcome gift" or, textually, a "morning gift" (*Morgengabe*) from Stalin to Hitler.

Wilhelm Mensing, author of a very comprehensive website on the fate of Germans expelled from the USSR and an acknowledged specialist on the issue, also does not corroborate this testimony:

> The present state of knowledge can be summarized as follows: there is no evidence of a contractual or quasi-contractual agreement in connection with the Hitler-Stalin Pact between the Pact States, Germany and the Soviet Union, on the departure of German prisoners from the Reich to Germany between 1939 and 1941, nor of such an agreement between the Gestapo and the NKVD during the preceding period, i.e., from 1937 onwards. Nor is there any evidence that these extraditions were motivated by the Soviet Union as an act of goodwill towards its Pact partner, Germany. There is no evidence of German involvement in the selection of persons to be deported (with the sole exception of an unsuccessful attempt by a small group); there are only indications of the (also largely unsuccessful) attempt by the German side to exclude certain prisoners (Jews, Communists) from extradition. There is nothing to indicate that Communists or others who felt "anti-fascist" were specifically selected by the Soviet camp for deportation.[9]

The Repression of Deported Peoples during the War

According to specialists in their field, historians Bugai and Gomov, "NKVD records attest that 180 convoy trains carrying 493,269 Chechen, Ingush and other nationalities departed at the same time. Fifty peo-

7 *Ibid.*

8 See among others: *Als Gefangene bei Stalin und Hitler. Eine Welt im Dunkel*, Ullstein, Munich, 2002 [1st ed., 1949, Verlag der Zwölf, Munich] [**Ed. Note:** Published in English as *Under Two Dictators: Prisoner of Stalin and Hitler*, Pimlico, 2008.].

9 Wilhelm Mensing, "Eine 'Morgengabe' Stalins an den Paktfreund Hitler?," *Zeitschrift des Forschungsverbundes SED-Staat*, no. 20, 2006.

ple died during the operation, and 1,272 died during the journey" (N. F. Bugai and A. M. Gomov, "The Forced Evacuation of the Chechens and the Ingush," Russian Studies in History, vol. 41, Fall 2002, no. 2, p. 43.) In Blood Lies, ch. 8, Grover Furr comments:

> This represents 0.27%, or 0.26% if you exclude the 50 people killed during disarmament, etc. This figure does not seem very high, since it occurred in winter, during the fiercest war in the history of the world. It is probably much lower than the rate suffered by Soviet civilians in the occupied zones.

As for the Crimean Tatars, out of the 151,720 sent to the Uzbek Soviet Socialist Republic in May 1944, 151,529 were registered by the NKVD of Uzbekistan, and 191 people died (0.13%) en route (cf. ref. p. 19). The high post-war mortality among these populations, often cited, is much more explained by the famine of 1946-1947, the last in Soviet history, which, of course, did not only affect these peoples (one to one and a half million deaths according to Australian historian S. Wheatcroft).

The massive collaboration of these populations with Nazi Germany did not allow them to be left behind the Red Army. In reality, deportation was a merciful measure. If the laws of war had been applied to the segment of the population that collaborated, these peoples probably would not have survived such a shock. Cross-reference with what Grover Furr says about it in *Khrushchev Lied*.

The German-Soviet Pact at the Origin of the Second World War?

This claim is nothing more than the thesis voted by the European Parliament (September 2019). On this matter, we refer to Ivan Maiski's classic *Who Helped Hitler* (*Qui aidait Hitler?*, Delga, 2014) about the manifest sabotage of the tripartite alliance (Franco-Anglo-Soviet), known as the "reverse alliance" by the Western bourgeoisies.

For his part, the historian Fadi Kassem had the good idea of pointing out a whole series of betrayals and compromises by the so-called "liberal democracies" which caused the anti-fascist alliance called for by the Soviets to fail and which, of course, the European Parliament preferred not to take into account when deciding on the responsibilities of the conflict. The list by Kassem was, however, significant:

1. Absence of reaction to the Japanese invasion of Manchuria in

China from September 1931, Japan being perceived as a bulwark against Bolshevism in Asia;

2. Absence of reaction to the reintroduction of compulsory military service in Germany in March 1935—a measure prohibited by the Treaty of Versailles of June 28, 1919;
3. French-English veto against the "reverse alliance" without truce proposed by the USSR in 1933, and then the pretended "Franco-Soviet Pact" of May 1935 sabotaged by the French (the one who signed this pact on the French side was... Pierre Laval! A real headache for the future collaborator...);
4. Anglo-German agreement of June 1935 allowing a powerful naval rearmament of Nazi Germany;
5. Contacts maintained and reinforced between the French (cf. Annie Lacroix-Riz, Le Choix de la défaite [The Choice of Defeat]) and British elites in particular with the German elites in the 1930s, to the point that former British Prime Minister Lloyd George, visiting the Führer's country house in Berchtesgaden in September 1936, declared about the latter: "Hitler does not dream of a Germany that threatens Europe. The Germans have lost all desire to enter into conflict with us" (cf. *Hitler, la folie d'un homme* [*Hitler, the folly of a man*], documentary, 2004);
6. Secret agreement between France and the United Kingdom and Fascist Italy (this is the Laval-Hoare Pact; we take this opportunity to point out Laval's attraction to Fascist regimes) to annex a large part of Ethiopia in May 1936—an action for which Italy was not sanctioned by the League of Nations (League of Nations) at the time...;
7. Remilitarization of the Rhineland in March 1936 (prohibited by the Treaty of Versailles);
8. War in Spain in which only the USSR and the International Brigades came to the aid of the Republican camp against Franco and his Fascist and Nazi allies, who operated in total complicity with the Reich and Italy;
9. Of course, the creation of the Anti-Komintern Pact mentioned above;
10. Anschluss (annexation of Austria by Germany) in March 1938, although prohibited by the Treaty of Versailles;

11. And most notably, the surrender of Czechoslovakia by France—although linked to Czechoslovakia by a treaty since 1924—and the United Kingdom, feeding Hitler's appetites after the signing of the shameful Munich Agreements in the night of September 29-30, 1938 (decision definitively taken in London by the British and the French on November 29, 1937, cf. Annie Lacroix-Riz, De Munich à Vichy [From Munich to Vichy]). It should be recalled that the USSR was absent from this agreement (and rightly so), unlike Fascist Italy which, like Nazi Germany, France and the United Kingdom, did not want the presence of the Soviets (or the Czechoslovaks, for that matter) at all.[10]

---

10 Fadi Kassem, "Il y a 80 ans, le pacte germano-soviétique: un symbole de l'histoire détournée par les réactionnaires!" [80 years ago, the German-Soviet Pact: a symbol of history diverted by reactionaries!"], *Initiative communiste*, August 2019.

Reply to Some Trotskyist Editors

On the Moscow Trials

While engaged in the translation and editing of an Italian book on Trotsky entitled *Le Vol de Piatakov. La collaboration tactique entre Trotsky et les nazis* [*Piatakov's Flight. The tactical collaboration between Trotsky and the nazis*],[1] I wanted to verify, for the purposes of accuracy, whether a French translation of the Dewey Commission report already existed. Indeed, the importance of this document with regard to the founder of the so-called Fourth International is known, since the Commission had met in April 1937 with Leon Trotsky in Coyoacán, not far from Mexico City, to interrogate the latter and implicitly allow him to respond to the accusations made against him by the Moscow Trials that were being carried out.

Thus, I discover that the French edition of this text (published in 1938 in English and available today in its entirety on the Internet in this language), far from being—curiously—a militant classic in the Trotskyist ranks in France, was not published in the language of Molière until 2018. It was through Éditions Syllepse (Paris) and Page 2 (Lausanne), which confirm on the back cover that this text published in 1938 had remained unpublished in French.

I would never have the audacity to think that this laudable but belated documentary effort could have been motivated by the recent

1 **Ed. Note:** Not translated into English at time of printing.

publications of the Delga editions, of which I am one of the responsible parties. Delga Editions, as one may know, has been rather reluctant to embrace the cult of personality surrounding Leon Trotsky.

However, I note that the preface to the French edition of the Dewey Commission, which we hope will be a historical presentation, rails against the Delga editions, said "neo-Stalinists," guilty of having published Grover Furr's books, namely *Les Amalgames de Trotsky* [*Trotsky's Amalgams*] and *Khrouchtchev a menti* [*Khrushchev Lied*]. I confess not to have understood what these people reproach Grover Furr with exactly, for the only excerpts quoted concern fourteen lines from the publisher's presentation (and this publisher is myself, dear editors, to speak without any vanity intended), lines described by the preface as, I quote, "the forgery of the forgery." These are the fourteen such scandalous lines of which I am the author, and which I have no trouble in republishing:

> Although previously purged of too compromising elements at the time of its opening to researchers in 1980, since then the Harvard Trotsky Archives have let leak certain unequivocal documents, such as the acknowledgements of the receipt of letters sent to defendants of the Moscow Trials, or even a letter from Leon Sedov to his father, Trotsky, evoking the creation of a conspiracy bloc uniting his supporters to the Zinovievists. Thus, eminent Sovietologists such as John Archibald Getty or the world-renowned Trotskyist historian Pierre Broué provided tangible and irrefutable proof of the existence of a Trotskyist plot in the USSR in the 1930s, a fact that Trotsky had always denied. [...] This book revolutionizes the understanding of the Moscow Trials. Trotsky's writings and activities in the 1930s must be reviewed in a new light, that of the latest machinations carried out by a brilliant and unscrupulous schemer, willing to do anything to return to power.

I also added some phrases that obviously did not catch the attention of my opponents:

> Drawing on primary sources from the Trotsky Archives, as well as the Soviet archives, Grover Furr subjects the testimony of the defendants in the Moscow Trials to a counter-investigation as close as possible to the sources. His conclusion: the confessions of the witnesses are authentic and concordant. The primary sources themselves, as well as Trotsky's writings, prove that the latter lied about almost everything concerning the USSR in his writings on the Moscow Trials (1936, 1937 and 1938), as well as about the assassination of Kirov, which he finally mentions in his testimony before the Dewey Commission in 1937.

There you have it. Delga Editions have published a book that dismantles, among other things, the conclusions of the Dewey Commission. An initiative that they refute with arguments from... the Dewey Commission. In the same involuntary comic genre, after the publication of Grover Furr's *Khrushchev Lied*, the Trotskyist historian Jean-Jacques Marie did not hesitate to republish... the Khrushchev Report! As for Edwy Plenel, he too had been indignant in an article in *Mediapart* against our publication, opposing it with the supposedly gospel truth of *My Life*, Leon Trotsky's autobiography. Anyway, we are going around in circles.

In my youth I knew Trotskyist militants whose alpha and omega about what they knew of the USSR was based on what Trotsky had wanted to write and nothing else, without any other element of comparison. This is the nature of sectarian thinking. However, I did not think I would find these defects in intellectuals of mature age.

My kind detractors at Éditions Syllepse and Page 2 go so far as to attribute to me a dispute about Pierre Broué, pretending not to understand what I meant, unless they themselves have understood nothing of what is really eroding the marble statue of their idol Leon Trotsky, in the current research.

I quote them, or rather I quote their preface, from Mr. Patrick Le Tréhondat:

> Adding a new layer of falsification to the falsification, historian Pierre Broué becomes, with this editor's note, the instrument of denunciation of a "Trotskyist plot in the USSR," when he has devoted his life to denouncing Stalinism and defending the ideas of Leon Trotsky"[2]

Rest assured, neither Furr nor his editor are unaware that Pierre Broué is a Trotskyist historian. Nevertheless, however much of a Trotskyist he may have been and remained to the end, and because he was above all a historian—which is entirely honorable—Pierre Broué was the one who brought to light exceptional documents found in the Trotsky Archives opened as of January 1980, and in particular the reconstitution of an opposition bloc, the existence of which Trotsky had always denied.

The article published in the 1980 *Cahiers Léon Trotsky* [*Leon Trotsky Notebooks*] is also available online.[3] Of course, Broué returns to it in his imposing 1988 biography of Trotsky, and in particular in the following chapter, entitled: "Groupings against Stalin in the USSR."

I never meant to say—because I do not share in any way, dear editors, your binary vision of things—that Broué has gone over to the so-

2 See p. 27 of Commission Dewey, *Trotsky n'est pas coupable* [Dewey Commission. *Trotsky is Not Guilty*], Syllepse/Page 2, Paris/Lausanne, 2018.

3 **Ed. Note:** They can be accessed at https://www.marxists.org/francais/clt/

called "Stalinist camp" or even "neo-Stalinist" (to use your terms), and that we would like to make him play a role obviously at the antipodes of his personality and his convictions. I simply say that he is the first of a series of historians who have contributed decisive elements on the clandestine pursuit of a very real Trotskyist activity, which Trotsky was at pains to deny, and which Broué praised, even in his last work devoted to the question, Communists against Stalin. Undoubtedly, this appreciation underestimates the risks of destabilization that these professional militants were running for a country besieged by the worst of the worst: the judgment recognizes the romantic aspect of this subversion but does not detect its Faustian sides. But that is just my humble opinion, and it is not the essential point.

The important thing is, I stress, do not underestimate the contradiction between what we know today and what we thought we knew at that time. So, dear editors, please update yourselves instead of continuing to present as revealed truth the report of the Dewey Commission where Trotsky falsely affirms—or rather falsely reaffirms because at the time he was quoting himself—the following:

> I have stated several times and I repeat it, that during the last nine years, Piatakov, like Radek [the two main defendants in the Second Moscow Trial], has not been my friend, but my bitterest and most perfidious enemy, and that there can be no negotiations between us. (p. 282, *op. cit.*).

In addition, on page 10 of the edition you put online, on the thirteenth and last session, Trotsky makes this interesting statement:

> However, even with regard to "negative facts," I cannot accept Professor Beard's overly categorical judgment. He assumes that, as an experienced revolutionary, I would not have kept documents that would have compromised me. This is absolutely true. Nevertheless, would I, in the most reckless and compromising manner, have written letters to the conspirators?

Yes, it is true: the idea of finding the slightest conspiratorial letter from Trotsky's hand was at that time highly improbable, even absurd. And, *a fortiori*, that of finding letters addressed to Piatakov and Radek with whom Trotsky, after the latter's adherence to Stalin, had severed all ties. And, even so. *E pur si muove*... And yet it moves; that is how the investigation progresses.

Following Broué, historian J. Arch Getty found the receipt of a letter from Trotsky sent to Radek, while the leader in exile considered the latter, as well as Piatakov, as "his bitterest and most perfidious enemy" to the point, he said, that there could be "no negotiations" between them.

It is known that Radek, one of the so-called "capitulators," that is, those who, like Piatakov, had renounced their Trotskyism after 1929 and had been integrated into the highest ranks of the Stalinist apparatus. Now, the letter dates from 1932, that is, long after Radek's official "abjuration" of Trotskyism. The latter had acknowledged in his trial the existence of this letter and even the place of receipt, Geneva. Proof of the double game played by this official "capitulator." Therefore, all we had at that time was Radek's "confession" at the Moscow Trials, categorically denied by Trotsky. I have been very careful to write "confession" in quotation marks, and I beg you to believe that I would not have wasted a minute of my time publishing works that would have adhered to the following simplistic and morally odious reasoning: "The accused are guilty, the proof is that they have confessed!" We know perfectly well that testimony can be extorted in different ways, including the most inquisitorial, under all regimes.

However, according to the editors the problem is that while the prosecution affirmed the existence of this letter and Trotsky denied it before the commission, no one could, in 1937, foresee that in 1986 an authoritative researcher, neither Trotskyist nor anti-Trotskyist, named John Archibald Getty, would discover in the Trotsky Archives the confirmation of the existence of this letter, after what Broué had already revealed. A reproduction of this receipt can be found in the Italian edition of *Il Volo di Pjatakov* [*Piatakov's Flight*], as well as in its French translation, which will be published in 2021.

It was necessary, then, due to the tenacity of Grover Furr and others to put this information from end to end and to have the courage to draw, along with many other elements from Russian sources, formidable consequences for the current conventional wisdom, at least these:

1. There was a clandestine opposition bloc (these are the words of Broué's article quoted above);
2. It came to involve even Radek and Piatakov, i.e. the upper echelons of the state;
3. The indictment was based on a real investigation, proof that, at least on these points, the "Stalinists" did not "shove" fanciful testimony down the defendants' throats.

In the same way, the researcher Sven-Eric Holström had shown that a classic refutation of Trotsky during the fourth session of this same Dewey Commission, which you published, came to nothing in the most complete way. It was that of the Bristol Hotel in Copenhagen. In fact, one of the defendants in the first trial, Holzman, another false "capitulator," had acknowledged having met Trotsky's son, Leon Sedov, at the Bristol Hotel in Copenhagen, in the prelude to a secret interview with Trotsky himself. On this, Trotsky had managed to prove that there was no Bristol Hotel near the Copenhagen station, nor anywhere else in Copenhagen.

End of the accusation? No, because there was a café "Bristol" near Copenhagen station, right next to a hotel with the impersonal name "Grand Hotel," which made it possible to confuse the one with the other, as Holzman probably did. Moreover, at the time, investigator Holström proved it: the two establishments communicated through a corridor (mentioned in the trial) and belonged to the same family. No matter how many quotation marks are put on Holzman's "confession," other corroborating evidence shows that the content of this confession is plausible, in any case not manipulated. And you will see, dear fellow editors, that Grover Furr brings in his latest book other very interesting research elements on the Bristol that I leave you to discover.

Similarly, you will be surprised by the book I am currently translating, *Le Vol de Piatakov. La collaboration tactique entre Trotsky et les nazis* [*Piatakov's Flight. The tactical collaboration between Trotsky and the nazis*], by Burgio, Leoni, and Sidoli.

In order to prepare you for your reading, possible now if you are reading in Italian, and in French if you are waiting for our edition in early 2021, I invite you to a small logic exercise based on his published work: in the sixth session, Trotsky seeks to dismantle the following accusation, made at the Second Moscow Trial.

Piatakov, whom Trotsky presented since his "capitulation"/denial—let us remember—as his bitterest enemy, had secretly met again with the latter, according to the accusation, and in December 1935 had taken advantage of an official trip to Germany at the time (a trip under tension given the evident hostility between the Nazi and Soviet regimes) to slip away for a day by plane, from Berlin to Oslo, in order to meet with Trotsky. This escape, given the possible control of the Soviet embassy in Berlin where Piatakov was staying, could only have happened with the complicity of the Nazi authorities.

Trotsky had weighed well what was at stake in such accusations. The text you publish contains an unequivocal statement by the founder of the Fourth International in this regard:

> If it were proved that Piatakov really visited me, my position would undoubtedly be compromised (p. 282).

Obviously, I will not reveal to you the research of the three shrewd Italians in order to leave you the pleasure of discovering it, but I can incite you from now on to verify what you yourselves published, that Trotsky had an armored alibi to dismantle this accusation. Except that the alibi was valid for the dates of December 20-22, which did not escape the attention of Dewey himself (you will verify it on page 288 of the work you publish), for the latter immediately pointed out to Trotsky that the statements of the accusation (the minutes of the Moscow Trial) did not refer to that date, but to December 11.

Small mistake, on the other hand, since Trotsky replied to Dewey at once that it was not the 11th, but the 10th. Which is true: Piatakov's testimony at the Moscow Trial clearly indicated the date of the 10th. This constitutes proof of the fact that, in spite of his fearsome intelligence, in rectifying a small error of Dewey's, Trotsky had there made a much more serious mistake, unintentionally revealing—and for posterity—that he was in fact perfectly aware of the date advanced by the prosecution, when at the same session he was endeavoring to propose a late alibi in the hope that the commission would not be too attentive to dates.

The most scandalous thing is that in the conclusions of the investigation, in this case at the thirteenth session, Trotsky dared to claim to have opposed an indestructible alibi to the thesis of Piatakov's flight. At the end of the Dewey Commission investigation, Trotsky had proved nothing!

This is just an example of what internal criticism of a document, in this case, yours, can reveal, even though, as I have pointed out, the critique of established historical truth can rely on many other corroborating pieces of evidence from other documents, such as the receipt for the letter sent to Radek that I mentioned earlier. They seem to be late because, in this respect, Radek's double-dealing with the Nazis is based on documents actually discussed since 1974. In this regard, we can consult an article by Grover Furr published in 1986 in the journal *Russian History*.

I would dare to remind you that the sabotages were confirmed by the American engineer—politician—John Littlepage, as early as 1938. You will also see in Annie Lacroix-Riz's book, *Le Choix de la défaite*

[*The Choice of Defeat*],[4] that the archives of numerous Western chancelleries show us from their opening that these chancelleries, and in particular the Foreign Office, were aware of Putna and Tukhachevsky's plot concerning the negotiation carried out in London with the Nazis on the overthrow of Stalin at the expense of Ukraine.

While waiting for you to update your information, we can nevertheless only congratulate you for making available this missing Trotskyist literature in French. For example, I have verified that the four articles written by Trotsky in 1939 for Ukrainian independence are available on the Internet in English, but not in French. It is a pity, because then our compatriots could measure the quality of the Trotskyist slogan of "unconditional defense" of the USSR against fascism. It is true that in his letter to Max Shachtman of September of the same year, available in French, Trotsky had reassured his comrade that this unconditional defense remained subordinate to the world view and interests of the Fourth International. Finally, let me conclude that, incredible as it may seem, the Moscow Trials, whose very term, as you rightly put it in your preface, has "passed into common parlance to designate a manipulative slanderous accusation," contain real and fearful elements of investigation. Perhaps it is the confusion between the trials and the time of the purges that followed—when, in this case, the authorities themselves recognized very serious errors, at least during the Yezhov trial—which explains this disorder in the minds and which became over time a real "epistemological obstacle."

The purges and their 700,000 victims (a figure no one disputes) are often described as the fruit of Stalin's alleged Neronian delirium. Clearly, a great fear had been instilled throughout the country, and it was precisely because the plots revealed in the Moscow Trials showed a real danger that the authorities believed in. Likewise, if one can legitimately speak of an overreaction in which paranoia is not absent, on the opposite side, laxity in the face of these dangers and of a Hitlerite invasion that was to cost the country 20 to 30 million dead—indeed, what would have become of the USSR and of the whole world if the Nazis had won?—was obviously, both for the time and now, unthinkable and morally unacceptable.

In conclusion, you have published a book where Trotsky had the merit of saying that on certain points, it was either Stalin or him who was right and that there is no middle ground. You will draw from these new

4 Armand Colin, Paris, 2006, pp. 393-396.

elements that I bring conclusions that suit you. I am not here to draw conclusions. I am not here to judge, let alone rejudge. My role is simply to facilitate the communication of information for readers, which unquestionably lacks and eludes you. It must be acknowledged that on numerous points, including in this text you publish as a response, one continues to discover that Trotsky lied.

December 16, 2020

KHRUSHCHEV LIED

JEAN-JACQUES MARIE OPTS FOR SLANDER

After the expected publication of *Khrushchev Lied* and a number of works on the history of the USSR, supported by recent research,[1] the cultivated public had the right to demand a debate on a par with the issues raised. Jean-Jacques Marie, whom we may regret does not have the same methodological scruples as his late comrade Pierre Broué, stuck to answering with slander and caricature.

I do not know if unmasking such procedures corresponds to the dignity of controversies among historians, and that is why I take the trouble to intervene as editor, to save this tedious task to the authors I publish.

In a work on the Khrushchev Report, recently published by Le Seuil,[2] Jean-Jacques Marie added to his translation of the report a presentation that ends with a full-fledged attack on the author of *Khrushchev Lied*, Grover Furr, as well as the author of its preface, Domenico Losurdo.

This prominent position, in conclusion to a tedious account of the ups and downs of the said report (without ever questioning its veraci-

1 Grover Furr, *Khrouchtchev a menti* [*Khrushchev lied*], Delga, Paris, 2014 (preface by Domenico Losurdo) and, recently: Grover Furr, *Le Massacre de Katyn. Une réfutation de la version "officielle"?* [*The Katyn Massacre. A refutation of the "official" version?*], Delga, Paris, 2015. See also Geoffrey ROBERTS, *Les Guerres de Staline. De la guerre mondiale à la guerre froide. 1939-1953* [*Stalin's Wars. From the World War to the Cold War. 1939-1953*], Delga, Paris, 2014 (preface by Annie Lacroix-Riz).

2 Jean-Jacques MARIE, *Le Rapport Khrouchtchev* [The Khrushchev Report], Le Seuil, Paris, September 2015.

ty), suggests that Jean-Jacques Marie intended to launch a counter-fire against these recent publications, categorically referred to here as a "Stalin defense attempt" without nuances. However, it was above all—and I proudly assume the publisher's share of responsibility—to defend the possibility of a history written without the prejudices of McCarthyism and the Cold War.

We would have liked to find in this field more sympathy and not vulgar *ad hominem* attacks against "that Furr" and "that Losurdo." Indeed, Jean-Jacques Marie, professor of classical letters, decided to use the demonstrative adjective ese, with a derogatory value. Be that as it may, one is astounded by Mr. Marie's contempt and nonchalance in summarizing the works of the American historian and the Italian philosopher:

> The gulag as a social elevator, the very humane deportation of peoples, Trotsky linked to the Nazis... the attempt to discredit Khrushchev's report in order to defend Stalin becomes a delusion.[3]

Goodness. What "delusion" is being referred to?

1. In one of his other works,[4] Domenico Losurdo shows, even when quoting the most anti-communist "official" historians (Anne Applebaum *in primis*), that the gulag was not at all an extermination machine (contrary to what the hateful assimilation of communism to Nazism would have us believe), but a penitentiary system in which there was the release of prisoners, remissions of sentences, and full reintegration into the social body. A statement, all in all measured, and one not well-suited for caricature.
2. With regard to the "very humane deportation of peoples," it is thus that J.J. Marie believes he can summarize the position of Grover Furr on the forced displacements of certain nationalities during the war, far from the Red Army's rearguard. Indeed, at the time, these populations represented a proven military danger, due to their past—and massive—collaboration with the Nazis. Furr underlines that if the laws of war—whether or not they seem too severe—had been applied, these populations would not have survived because of the penalties that would

3 *Ibid.* p. 75.

4 Domenico Losurdo, *Staline. Histoire et critique d'une légende noire* [Stalin. History and critique of a black legend], Aden, Brussels, 2011. [**Ed. Note:** Published in English translation in 2023, Iskra Books.]

have been legally imposed on the male population that had directed their weapons against the USSR. It was thus a measure of clemency, linked to the concern of the Soviets to ensure the survival of the various nationalities. The number of deaths, inevitably provoked by these emergency forced displacements, is astonishingly low in such a context if one compares the archival data provided by Furr with the fantastic figures given by Jean-Jacques Marie without the slightest documentary note.

3. "Trotsky linked to the Nazis": Grover Furr has provided numerous elements in this regard, so I can only refer to these works and articles in English, in addition to the work we have published.[5] It seems that a complete book on the subject is being published. However, to stick to the national level, it is established that the French Trotskyists preferred to ally themselves in the midst of the Cold War with the worst of the time—the CIA—to form an anti-CGT union. Other previous alliances with other imperialists, and in different countries, are not surprising. Mrs. Annie Lacroix-Riz also provided Mr. Marie, in 2007, with archival references attesting to the collaboration of numerous French Trotskyists during the war.[6] For the time being, the latter has not deigned to respond to her proposal for arbitration concerning the interpretation to be given to these documents.

It does not behoove a modest editor to remind Jean-Jacques Marie that his militant commitment should not prevail on his duties as a historian. We can only hope that the serenity of the debate prevails over this way of making history with truncheons and feigned indignation. Because "no one," says the philosopher, "lies as much as the indignant."

September 2015

5 See: https://msuweb.montclair.edu/~furrg/

6 See http://www.reveilcommuniste.fr/article-annie-lacroix-riz-repond-a-l-historien-trotskyste-jean-jacques-marie-biographe-de-staline-55479078.html.

Refusing Trotsky's Storytelling

Would That be Considered Denialism?
A Reply to Edwy Plenel[1]

"Anything excessive is insignificant," Talleyrand is reported to have said, and, despite your exaggerations, Edwy, you have not succeeded in eliciting from me more than a shrug of the shoulders.

Your article is tantamount to being outraged by the fact that there are still communists who refuse to contribute to the only version of communism still tolerated by the current power, that of Trotskyism—the minority worldwide.

You claim to oppose historical research with 'a truth' contained in the Memoirs of Leon Trotsky.

Is it a book of revelation, and should we think that we have committed blasphemy?

You do not bother engaging with any argument of Grover Furr's book, *Trotsky's Amalgams*, which you reproache us for having published. You admit to having "skimmed" it, which means that you have not really read it. And you have only one argument: it is nothing less than denialism.

---

1 **Ed. Note:** Edwy Plenel (born 1952) is a French political journalist, working for *Le Monde* and *Mediapart* as well as Trotskyist publications such as *Rouge*.

I know perfectly well that the existence of communists who do not submit to the blackmail of what historian Annie Lacroix-Riz calls "the anti-Sovietism of comfort" has always constituted a kind of scandal for the supporters of the so-called Fourth International.

Nevertheless, through the invention of an improbable "Stalinist" denialism, and an implicit comparison with the Faurisson's denial of the existence of the gas chambers in the Nazi camps, you intend to arouse indignation and above all to intimidate, for example, the management of *L'Humanité*, which you judge guilty of hosting our editions, as if it were up to you to choose your guests. This insult to the intelligence of your readers is not very surprising in these times when the absurd comparison between Nazism and Stalinism has just been confirmed and validated by the European Parliament (September 19, 2019), by all political tendencies, from the extreme right to the ecologist and social-democrat deputies via the Macronists. However, it is tantamount to putting on the same plane those who have committed genocide and those who have put an end to it, those who have subjected the Slavic peoples to slavery and decadence and those who, on the contrary, from the voice of their leader, affirmed fighting: "The Hitlers come and go; the German people remain."

You are the author of the preface to *My Life*. Trotsky is God and Plenel is his prophet. Why not? The 20th century will be religious, Malraux said, and you give a rather unexpected example.

I simply hope, considering the passionate relationship you maintain with such a sacred book, that you are not on the path of radicalization, as it is currently expressed. Judging by the relational finesse that Mediapart demonstrates in writing articles about one of our authors who has already undergone four days of police custody, I dare not imagine how far your purifying fury could take you. I also dare not think about how far your will—undoubtedly "anti-totalitarian"?—to *a priori* define, based on your preferences, the tolerable limits of the debate, democratically excluding the communists who displease you, will carry you.

Regarding another judicial scandal related to the climate of war maintained by our so-called Western democracies, you were kind enough to mention the book I wrote about Julian Assange, *Julian Assange en danger de mort* [*Julian Assange in danger of death*].

However, I have not seen you, at Mediapart, motivated by this cause. Are judicial errors only interesting when they can be attributed to Joseph Stalin?

If you did not claim to settle, all by yourself, the controversies between the Third and the so-called Fourth International, I believe you could devote more time to defending your Australian colleague and what he represents for the entire journalism profession.

However, to get back to the substance of Professor Furr's book, I advise you to go beyond just skimming through it, even if it clashes with your prejudices.

You will see that the gist of the book is founded on the Trotsky Archives opened in 1980, and also on the conclusions drawn from them by the most world-renowned Trotskyist historian, Pierre Broué, the only one who has carried his commitment (dare we say "obstinacy") to the point of fully assuring what his archives contained, namely the existence of a "1932 Opposition Bloc." This reality emerged from the Trotsky Archives despite a thorough censorship (traces of which still remain, even in the expurgated archives) and which testify to what Trotsky had always denied (this is the first "denial"): the reality of a seditious internal opposition.

No biographer of Trotsky has gone so far since then. They have all backed down and preferred to keep quiet about what those files contained.

So, it is to the memory of Pierre Broué, the foremost Trotskyist specialist on Trotsky, that you should somehow address yourself, as he was one of the first to establish that the thesis of the "pathology" of Stalin as the sole cause of the Moscow trials was not plausible. And this, in the following terms:

> The same comments could be made about the 1932 bloc of oppositionists that other researchers have perceived, without recognizing it, for lack of a sufficient chronological tool or because of solid prejudices and preconceived ideas. How to explain the difficulty of giving this discovery the publicity it deserved? The first echo of the 1980 article mentioning the bloc and reproducing the documents attesting to it is by the American Arch J. Getty and dates from 1985. However, the opposition bloc had already begun a revision of the classic histories of Soviet Russia. In fact, it modifies the pathological image of Stalin as the key to development and leads us rather to the economic difficulties, to the social and political conflicts, to the struggle for power, rather than to the simple bloodlust of the "tyrant" (Pierre Broué, *Trotsky*, 1988, Fayard, ch. 48).

To our knowledge, until Grover Furr's present book, silence regarding the "bloc of oppositionists" or Sedov's invisible-ink letter to Trotsky announcing the formation of a conspiracy has persisted, even among Trotsky's biographers, who may not share the same rigor in archival research, presumably. Isaac Deutscher, despite having had access to the archives before they were opened, had not mentioned it either, but this is hardly surprising, as Trotsky was already, for him, a "prophet," as indicated by the title of the reverent biography he dedicated to him.

Finally, let us recall that "negationism" is a crime when it concerns the verdict of the Nuremberg Trials. Applying the slanderous and defamatory term "negationism" without examination to research on the Stalinist era is begging the question, because through the publication of this book, we have never denied anything else but the Immaculate Conception and Pontifical Infallibility of Leon Trotsky's supporters. In reality, I have not encountered any historian, author, or intellectual to date who denies the existence of the gulag or the famine in Ukraine.

I have never published such "denialism," or rather such foolishness.

It is also worth remembering that, whatever the causes of the famine of the early 1930s, it was the last in Russian and Soviet history, and it was collectivization that put an end to these tragedies. Finally, let us remember that today's triumphant capitalism is very well suited, as Jean Ziegler, former UN rapporteur on the right to food, says, to the fact that today a child dies every five seconds from hunger or the causes of famine. I believe that it is above all the denial of this tragically contemporary scandal that we are facing.

Personally, I have never practiced what has been erroneously called the "cult of personality," which on the other hand would have been necessary to translate, to be exact, as the "cult of the person." However, I consider that, as a communist, one should not lend one's flank to caricature and/or slander, nor to the cult of Trotsky or the demonization of Stalin: the latter is certainly criticizable, even harshly and on the basis of factual arguments, but one cannot take away from him the fact that he was the main victor over Hitler, as General De Gaulle recalled in 1944 when he declared: "The French know what Soviet Russia did for them, and they know that it was precisely Soviet Russia that played the leading role in their liberation." If the Holocaust was repressed, if millions of Jews and Slavs survived in Europe, if today we can dispute freely (and, no doubt, too freely for their taste?), we owe it in part to them. Just as no one disagrees, we also owe in part to Trotsky the victory of the Red Army over the White Army.

My commitment as author and editor remains to a full and complete democracy, which in no way denies the so-called formal rights. These rights come not only from the bourgeois revolutions, as is often believed, but also and mainly, in terms of their international dimension (UN Charter, Universal Declaration of Human Rights), from the victory of the Red Army in 1945, under the leadership of Joseph Stalin. It is important to remember this. To these formal rights I consider that we must urgently add the rights that derive concretely from socialism, starting with the right not to die of hunger, not to immolate oneself by fire because all hope is lost, and the duty not to exploit others.

On the other hand, what could constitute denialism on his part, would be to make people believe that the Moscow Trials that testify to sabotage and attempts to destabilize the Soviet regime, promoted mainly by Hitlerite Germany, have no other foundation than Stalin's alleged paranoia, which at the very least feeds a childish view of the politics and intentions of the Reich in particular. I recall that, at the time, even the U.S. ambassador was convinced of the veracity of the Moscow Trials. For my part, this in no way means that I validate the expeditious manner in which they were carried out, but it is necessary to take into account the international context, that of the rise of fascism and militarism, not only throughout Europe, but also in Japan.

In *Le Choix de la défaite* [*The Choice of Defeat*], historian Annie Lacroix-Riz provides numerous details, supported by archives for which she provides references, especially regarding the Tukhachevsky conspiracy. If you wish to delve into the details, it is not impossible that Grover Furr might also respond, even though no historical arguments have been raised by you so far.

I had already responded to Mr. Jean-Jacques Marie in the same way in a previous controversy, saying that historians would respond when the discussion rises above the simple polemic between publicists.

Sensing that neither you nor I will definitively settle any of these important questions, I bid farewell. However, I hope to find in you a more attentive ear regarding the fate of Julian Assange, for which we are all civically responsible. Not to mention Mumia Abu-Jamal, who is slowly dying in a U.S. prison after a notoriously rigged trial. As Epictetus said, there is fundamentally what depends on us and what does not. Assange is our concern; let's talk about it instead of implicitly seeking to invoke censorship, with cries of *negationism!* against one of the rare French publishers who continue to publish Marxists, not all of whom, incidentally, share Grover Furr's positions.

Awaiting your response on this urgent matter, I have the honor to remain, sir, your friendly interlocutor.

February 2020

It is Better to Laugh

Or, the Obsessions of Thierry Wolton[1]

A Ghost Haunts Wolton

From the time when communism was already haunting Europe, we can see that in the matter of polemical outbursts, His Holiness Pope Pius IX, describing the communists and other modernists as "drink[ing] the poison of the serpent in the goblet of Babylon," had set the bar very high, so to speak, at the outset. The inquisitorial style still finds in our contemporaries some epigones. Thus, we had already been struck by Thierry Wolton's books against communism, truly grotesque enormities because of their voluntarily exaggerated and involuntarily comical character. From their title, one notices that Mr. Wolton took Hegel's famous statement "the world's history is the world's court of judgment" a little too literally.

In fact, his recent trilogy—*Histoire Mondiale du Communisme I. Les Bourreaux* [World History of Communism I. The Executioners]; *Histoire Mondiale du Communisme II Les Victimes* [World History of Communism II. The Victims]; and *Histoire Mondiale du Communisme III. Les Complices* [World history of Communism III; The Accomplices]—reveals that this is a polemical literature that will certainly delight enthusiasts but whose reading does not appear particularly essential to the scientific debate.

1 **Ed. Note:** Thierry Wolton (born 1952) is a French anti-communist historian.

Life in Red and Brown

I was considering, for a while, delving into an earlier work by the same author dealing with the so-called "red-brown" phenomenon, wanting to understand what factual basis could support such an aberration or oxymoron. I now think I can do without it, given that Mr. Wolton's latest opus, dedicated to the "left-wing denialists," shows that this epithet means absolutely nothing, as Mr. Wolton deems it fitting like a glove, and even in a "classic" manner—my goodness!—for my comrade and friend Georges Gastaud, characterized as a "nostalgic of Stalinism, coupled with a fierce nationalist, in a classic red-brown mixture."

Mr. Wolton could have read, before spouting his nonsense, the work *Marxisme et Universalisme* [*Marxism and Universalism*] by Georges Gastaud. He would have seen, through analyses imbued with high Marxist culture, that the philosopher renews internationalism as properly understood, i.e., cooperation among nations.

Is speaking of the nation, even in the internationalist framework, something suspicious in Mr. Wolton's eyes, from the outset? Does he feel bold enough to call the third article of the Declaration of the Rights of Man and of the Citizen of 1789, according to which the principle of all sovereignty rests essentially on the nation, "red-brown"?

Let's also recall that Georges Gastaud is one of the first, representing the PRCF[2] since 2004, to have revisited in programmatic terms the National Council of the Resistance, incessantly emphasizing that this program excluded by principle the two main culprits of collaboration, namely big business and... the far right.

As for the alleged nostalgia for Stalinism, it is notorious that Georges Gastaud was never one of those Marxist-Leninists always adept at the cult of personality, and he always claimed the critical examination of the entire history of communism, including the errors of what he rightly calls "primosocialism." It can be seen in all his works. So, does Mr. Wolton read the works he is talking about? It is to be hoped for Mr. Wolton that Georges Gastaud takes this with humor and does not take it to the legal arena.

2 **Ed. Note:** *Pôle de Renaissance Communiste en France* [*Pole of Communist Revival in France*], a French communist political party founded in 2004.

I Have Denied Goebbels; is it Serious, Doctor?

In the same laughable book by Mr. Wolton, your humble servant is personally blamed as responsible for the publication of books deemed negationist. I would, for example, make the mistake of editing a book characterizing the Katyn massacres as a "Nazi crime."

On this point, I plead guilty and with pleasure. After reading (and editing) Grover Furr's book *The Mystery of the Katyn Massacre: The Evidence, the Solution*, I consider myself convinced of the fact that Joseph Goebbels' thesis, according to which it was the Soviets and not the Nazis who executed several thousand Polish prisoners in the Katyn forest, can be rightly denied.

One can only arrive at the opposite conclusion by giving credence to the documents handed over by Yeltsin to the Polish government, which notably includes a blatant forgery: a letter from Stalin to Beria dated 1940 with the stamp of the Central Committee of the CPSU, the name of the Communist Party that only came into use from... 1952. Such a conclusion can only be reached by denying the discoveries of the Volodymyr-Volynskyi mass grave (2011-2012), the site of massacre of Western Ukrainian populations by the SS. Investigators exhumed there two insignias of Polish soldiers allegedly executed, according to the so-called official version... 1,200 kilometers from there. This discovery led to the immediate cessation of searches by Ukrainian and Polish authorities.

Such a conclusion can only be reached by crediting the Nazi report, which was visibly drawn up in such haste that, for example, it gives an account of a letter written in German by a Polish soldier to a camp director, proving that Polish prisoners had passed through a Nazi camp before their execution.

The author—and his humble French publisher—are therefore eagerly awaiting challengers. For now, we mostly encounter the outraged, not the challengers. Something else: our editions would like, according to Mr. Wolton, to make believe that "the Great Terror is a coup staged by Yezhov." We owe the expression "Great Terror" to IRD agent Robert Conquest, who used it instead of what the Soviets called the "Yezhovshchina" (the "dirty Yezhov period"). I gladly concede that Yezhov cannot be held solely responsible for this whole period (1937-1938), but I would like to know what evidence can be presented to postulate the latter's innocence and the necessity of dealing with Soviet history in English and not in Russian.

As a general rule, it is curious to note that the will to establish a denialism for the Stalinist era leads, whether consciously or not, to whitewash the Nazi maneuvers. Indeed, according to the dominant ideology, it would be denialist to claim that the Moscow Trials have the slightest foundation. So, the Nazis never tried to sabotage Soviet industry between 1933 and 1941, never tried to advance their pawns as they did in France via the example of Otto Abetz or other agents?

Let us continue. According to Mr. Wolton, Delga editions would deny the truths established by the Khrushchev Report. This statement, without further precision, allows the layman to believe that we would deny certain facts such as the existence of the penitentiary system called gulag (of which, however, the report does not speak). On the other hand, are we to believe Khrushchev's word when he describes Stalin directing his armies by means of a simple world map, that is to say, without the use of General Staff maps? This fact contradicts the testimonies of Churchill, Harriman and so many others as to Stalin's military competence.

We are, finally, accused of contesting, through our editorial actions, the scale of the victims of the famine in Ukraine in 1932-1933. This is inaccurate: the book published by us, authored by Mark Tauger, an undisputed specialist in Soviet agriculture, simply questions the artificial nature of the famine while demonstrating that collectivization ended it. Once again, it is regrettable to note that Mr. Wolton does not read the books he talks about.

When the Boundaries of Grotesqueness are Surpassed

Clearly, Mr. Wolton judges these works by the title that appears on their covers. He also seems to like to attack the dead (Domenico Losurdo, Jean Salem), unless he doesn't even know that the latter, unfortunately, are no longer able to answer him. Or he strikes blindly and randomly on everything that moves under the umbrella of Delga Editions. Likewise, if we believe our polemicist, Vladimiro Giacché is considered guilty of having inspired Mr. Jean-Luc Mélenchon and would not have the right to qualify the annexation of the GDR as a "Second Anschluss," since reunification is, according to Wolton, nothing but a road paved with roses. The same goes for Monika Karbowska, whom our effervescent contradictor reproaches for feeling nostalgia for people's Poland. It is difficult to understand why this would be denialism, or should we understand that this foolish French-Polish historian deserves a good psychoanalysis to stop this intolerable denial of her martyred childhood in socialist Poland? As we see with the latter, this pursuit of denialism takes a truly obsessive turn in Mr. Wolton. It is true that these historians who deny revealed truths are tiresome. There is also the example of Annie Lacroix-Riz, whom Mr. Wolton reproaches for her "hypercriticism." Another fool! Who said that history has to be critical?

All we can wish for our polemicist, therefore, is to take it easy on his sore brain due to these untimely critiques, to take a little rest, while offering a piece of advice: before writing, one must first know how to *read*. As for us, we will choose to laugh about it, as this controversy does no one any favors. The only thing that consoles us in this matter is to see our catalog implicitly contested by our colleagues at the Grasset publishing house. They always find it useful to bear the name of their founder, who was condemned after the war for national degradation.[3] By making the modest Delga Editions their antagonist they have, all in all, not made a bad choice.

February 2, 2020

---

3 **Ed. Note:** "National Demotion" (*dégradation nationale*) was a penalty instituted in France following the liberation of the country after WW2. It was utilized as part of the legal purging that ensued after the downfall of the Vichy regime. The *dégradation nationale* was among the sentences that the Courts of Justice could impose. Its purpose was to sanction offenses of "national unworthiness" (*Indignité nationale*).

To Michel Onfray, War Propagandist

20 MILLION DEATHS,
THESE ARE NOT THE DEATHS OF THE GULAG;
THEY ARE THE SOVIET VICTIMS OF NAZI BARBARISM.

We came across *Décadence* [*Decadence*][1] a bit by chance during a train journey. One of the first marks of "decadence" in our country is precisely that one of the few vaguely theoretical books that can be bought in a large station is none other than Onfray's latest pensum. The other manifest "decadence" is that of the Flammarion editions and, no doubt, of bourgeois publishing in general, incapable of forcing an author to reread himself, such is the quantity of factual errors and inaccuracies.

Sometimes these are simple typos, which only serve to demonstrate the author's negligence and casualness (for example, when he wants to evoke the racist cliché of the Aryan "brachycephalic" and not "dolichocephalic."[2]

Sometimes the error is more serious, especially when one pretends to review twenty centuries of the history of Christianity as a connoisseur: Onfray thus claims that the Essenes disappeared "without leaving

1 Michel Onfray. *Décadence: Vie et mort du judéo-christianisme*. Paris: Flammarion, 2017.

2 *Ibid.*, p. 45.

traces or texts."[3] And the *Dead Sea Scrolls*?

Sometimes the error is a voluntary provocation, in "the-more-exorbitant-the-more-convincing" mode, for example: "the 20 million dead of the gulag."[4]

It is precisely on this point that we would like to dwell, since the book hardly deserves superfluous comments.

After delivering the enormity of 20 million deaths, intended to forever discredit any inclination to establish socialism and to prompt us toward a Schopenhauerian cynicism, Onfray does not provide us with any sources in footnotes. And for good reason.

The figures of the gulag, since the opening of the Archives in 1990, have not been contested by anyone. Often noted as GARF (Russian acronym for the State Archives of the Russian Federation), these researches have been conducted and supported by specialists who cannot be credited with partisan intentions, certainly not communist (Zemskov, Khlevniouk, Getty, Rittersporn, etc.).

Relying—like everyone else—on these works, in *The Black Book of Communism*, which is entirely designed as an indictment (to the point of "forgetting" to mention foreign intervention, especially French, during the so-called civil war), the nonetheless very anti-communist Nicolas Werth speaks of 300,000 deaths in Soviet camps between 1934 and 1940 (pocket edition, p. 294). Werth then mentions 249,000 deaths for 1942 and 167,000 in 1943 (*Ibid*. p. 321), the wartime period when it is difficult to attribute the victims to the regime, at a time when the Soviets were dying—this time by millions—as a result of the Hitlerian invasion.

The figures for death sentences during the Stalinist period are also known (and uncontested): 720,000 people, of which 680,000 were for the period 1937-1938.[5] The debates rather focus on whether or not to contest the Soviet version attributing these excesses mainly to the machinations of Ezhov and Frinovsky, who were replaced by Beria, who, contrary to popular belief, would put an end to this repression.

Contingents of victims that contribute, particularly in the case of China, to the relentless propaganda of *The Black Book* are attributed to

3 *Ibid.*, p. 57.

4 *Ibid.*, p. 447.

5 *Cf. The Black Book of Communism*, p. 294.

famines blamed on the regime, following the implicit rule: when there is a famine in a capitalist or feudal regime, it's blamed on the climate; in a communist regime, it's blamed on the communists, and why not on Voltaire and Rousseau, on the "gulag already in Marx, or even in Plato," etc. We are not told anything, for example, about the famine in Niger concurrent with the one in Ukraine, even though Niger was then part of French West Africa (A.O.F.). Nor are we told that it is under communist regimes, especially in China and Russia, that the specter of famine has definitively receded, with China, thanks to the communists, transforming from an ultra-poor country after the Opium Wars to almost the leading economic power today, etc.

Therefore, one should respond to Michel Onfray that 20 million deaths are not the victims of the gulag; they are the Soviet victims of Nazi barbarism, at least on the lower end of the estimate, with variations between 20 and 30 million (including 3 million Soviet prisoners who died of hunger and mistreatment).

For a certain Adolf Hitler, the "Judeo-Bolsheviks" had killed 30 million people in Russia. This imaginary figure from *Mein Kampf* would, ironically enough, become the number of deaths caused by his own intervention, intended to turn Russia into the "German Indies."

On page 78 of his work, Onfray makes a dubious comparison between Christianity and Nazism, arguing that *Mein Kampf* admires the passage from the Gospels about the money changers in the temple. One must have a particularly twisted mind to endorse such a comparison and think that a passing citation from a universally known text proves anything.

However, no one thinks to highlight the commonalities in anti-communist hatred between Onfray and the Nazi leader, up to this disturbing similarity in the numbers of anti-communist propaganda, to this strange accusatory inversion intended to attribute to Stalin the number of deaths that Hitler caused in the USSR.

It is true that the record had long been broken, and it seems that in the realm of anti-communism, the boundaries of plausibility have been crossed: for the late Solzhenitsyn, 110 million Russians fell victim to Stalinism (*cf.* his speech in March 1976 in Spain justifying the continuation of Franco's regime).

After all, when one enters such logic, anything becomes possible. Even suggesting bombing communist countries, even if it leads to nuclear apocalypse.

Onfray is indeed on the verge of taking that step and turning into Dr. Strangelove.

All of this is happening on public television. In a program entirely dedicated to someone who willingly presents himself as a pariah (France 2, January 10, 2017), interviewed by Léa Salamé, who reproaches him for not applying the right to interfere in Muslim countries with enough zeal, Onfray retorts:

> If your doctrine is that we need to oust dictators, I invite you to go bomb North Korea, go bomb China, go bomb Cuba, go bomb a number of places where indeed human rights are violated and massacred, and surprisingly, you'll see that there will never be anyone willing to send bombs there.

Trifles for a massacre? It seems that's what it means to be left-wing.

January 2017

Works Cited

Alleg, Henri. *Le Grand Bond en arrière* [*The Great Leap Backwards*]. Paris: Delga, 2008.

Applebaum, Anne. *Gulag: A History*. New York: Penguin, 2004.

———. R*ed Famine: Stalin's War on Ukraine*. Doubleday, 2017.

Blackmon, Douglas. *Slavery By Another Name: The Re-enslavement of Black Americans from the Civil War to World War II*. New York: Anchor Books, Random House, 2008.

Bloch, Marc. *L'étrange défaite: témoignage écrit en 1940* [*The Strange Defeat: Testimony Written in 1940*]. Paris: Folio Histoire, 1994.

Bugai, N. F., and A. M. Gomov. "The Forced Evacuation of the Chechens and the Ingush." *Russian Studies in History* 41 (Fall 2002).

Broué, Pierre. *Trotsky*. Paris: Fayard, 1988.

Buber-Neumann, Margarete. *Als Gefangene bei Stalin und Hitler. Eine Welt im Dunkel*. Munich: Ullstein, 2002 [1st ed. 1949, Verlag der Zwölf, Munich].

Burgio, Daniel, Massimo Leoni, and Roberto Sidoli. *Il Volo di Pjatakov. La Collaborazione tattica tra Trotsky e i nazis*. Milan: Pgreco, 2017.

Colley, Margaret Siriol. *More than a Grain of Truth: The Biography of Gareth Jones*. Edited by Nigel Linsan Colley, 2005.

Courtois, Stéphane, et al. *The Black Book of Communism*. Paris: Robert Laffont, 1997.

Danilov, V. P. Коллективизация: как это было, Страницы истории советского общества: факты, проблемы, люди. Moscow, 1989.

Davies, Robert W., and Stephen G. Wheatcroft. *The Years of Hunger: Soviet Agriculture, 1931-1933*. New York: Palgrave Macmillan, 2004.

Deutscher, Isaac. *Trotsky I. Le prophète armé, 1879-1921* [*Trotsky I. The Armed Prophet, 1879-1921*]. Paris: Omnibus, 1996.

Duguet, Raymond. *Un bagne en Russie rouge* [*A Prison in Red Russia*]. Preface by Nicolas Werth, 2004.

Ferro, Marc, ed. *Le livre noir du colonialisme* [*The Black Book of Colonialism*]. Paris: Robert Laffont, 2003.

Furr, Grover. *Khrouchtchev a menti* [*Khrushchev Lied*]. Preface by Domenico Losurdo. Paris: Delga, 2014.

———. *Les Amalgames de Trotsky* [*Trotsky's Amalgams*]. Paris: Delga, 2015.

———. *L'énigme du massacre de Katyn. Les preuves. La solution* [*The Mystery of the Katyn Massacre: The Evidence, the Solution*]. Paris: Delga, 2019 (an earlier work, *Le massacre de Katyn. Une réfutation de la version "officielle"* [*The Katyn Massacre: A Refutation of the "Official" Version*], was published in 2015 by the same publisher).

———. *Blood Lies: The Evidence that Every Accusation against Joseph Stalin and the Soviet Union in Timothy Snyder's "Bloodlands" Is False*. Red Star Publishers, 2014.

Gastaud, Georges. *Marxisme et Universalisme* [*Marxism and Universalism*]. Paris: Delga, 2015.

Getty, John A. *Origins of the Great Purges: The Soviet Communist Party Reconsidered, 1933-1938*. New York: Cambridge University Press, 1985.

Getty, J. A., G. T. Rittersporn, and V. N. Zemskov. "Les victimes de la répression pénale dans l'URSS d'avant-guerre" [The Victims of Penal Repression in the Prewar USSR]. *Revue des études slaves* 65 (1993): 631-670.

Getty, J. A., and R. T. Manning. *Stalinist Terror, New Perspectives.* Cambridge, 1993.

Giacché, Vladimiro. *Le Second Anschluss, l'annexion de la RDA: L'unification de l'Allemagne et l'avenir de l'Europe* [*The Second Anschluss, the Annexation of the GDR: The Unification of Germany and the Future of Europe*]. Paris: Delga, 2015.

Harrison, Mark. *Soviet Planning in Peace and War 1938-1945.* Cambridge: University Press, 1985.

———. *The Economics of World War II: Six Great Powers in International Comparison.* Cambridge: Cambridge University Press, 1998.

———. *Accounting for War: Soviet Production, Employment, and the Defence Burden, 1940-1945.* Cambridge: Cambridge University Press, 1996.

Karbowska, Monika. *De la Pologne populaire à l'hiver capitaliste* [*From Popular Poland to the Capitalist Winter*]. Paris: Delga, 2018.

Kassem, Fadi. "Il y a 80 ans, le pacte germano-soviétique: un symbole de l'histoire détournée par les réactionnaires!" [80 Years Ago, the German-Soviet Pact: A Symbol of History Diverted by Reactionaries!]. *Initiative communiste*, August 2019.

Kokurin, A. I., and Iu. N. Morukov, eds. *Stalinskie Stroïki GULAGA 1930-1953*, Dokumenty. Moscow: MDF—"Materik," 2005.

Kotkin, Stephen. *Stalin: Waiting for Hitler* (1929-1941). Penguin, 2017.

Lacroix-Riz, Annie. *Le Choix de la défaite, Les élites françaises dans les années 30* [*The Choice of Defeat, French Elites in the 1930s*]. Paris: Armand Colin, 2006, 2nd ed. 2010.

———. *De Munich à Vichy: l'assassinat de la Troisième République, 1938-1940* [*From Munich to Vichy: The Assassination of the Third Republic, 1938-1940*]. Paris: Armand Colin, 2008.

———. *Le Vatican, l'Europe et le Reich, de la Première guerre mondiale à la guerre froide* [*The Vatican, Europe and the Reich, from the First World War to the Cold War*]. Paris: Armand Colin, 1996, 2nd ed.

2010.

Losurdo, Domenico. Staline. *Histoire et critique d'une légende noire* [*Stalin. History and Critique of a Black Legend*]. Brussels: Aden, 2011.

Maiski, Ivan. *Qui aidait Hitler* [*Who Helped Hitler*]. Paris: Delga, 2014.

Marie, Jean-Jacques. *Le Rapport Khrouchtchev* [*The Khrushchev Report*]. Paris: Le Seuil, 2015.

Mensing, Wilhelm. "Eine 'Morgengabe' Stalins an den Paktfreund Hitler?" *Zeitschrift des Forschungsverbundes SED-Staat 20* (2006).

Monville, Aymeric. *Julian Assange en danger de mort* [*Julian Assange in Danger of Death*]. Paris: Delga, 2019.

Ohayon, Isabelle. *La sédentarisation des Kazakhs dans l'URSS de Staline. Collectivisation et changement social (1928-1945)* [*The Sedentarization of the Kazakhs in Stalin's USSR. Collectivisation and Social Change (1928-1945)*]. Preface by Nicolas Werth. Paris: Maisonneuve et Larose, 2005.

Onfay, Michel. *Décadence* [*Decadence*]. Paris: Flammarion, 2017.

Orwell, George. *Animal Farm*. London: Secker and Warburg, 1945.

Perrault, Gilles. *Review of The Black Book of Communism*. Le Monde diplomatique, December 1997.

Roberts, Geoffrey. *Les Guerres de Staline. De la guerre mondiale à la guerre froide, 1939-1953* [*Stalin's Wars. From the World War to the Cold War, 1939-1953*]. Preface by Annie Lacroix-Riz. Paris: Delga, 2014.

Suing, Guillaume. *Évolution: la preuve par Marx. Dépasser la légende noire de Lyssenko* [*Evolution: The Proof by Marx. Overcoming the Black Legend of Lysenko*]. Preface by Georges Gastaud. Paris: Delga, 2016.

———. *L'écologie réelle: une histoire soviétique et cubaine* [*Real Ecology: A Soviet and Cuban History*]. Preface by Viktor Dedaj. Paris: Delga, 2018.

———. "Lysenko: un imposteur?" [Lysenko: An Imposter?]. *Investig'action*, May 10, 2016.

Tauger, Mark. *Famine et transformation agricole en URSS* [*Famine and Agricultural Transformation in the USSR*]. Paris: Delga, 2017.

Tchouev, Félix. *Conversations with Molotov: 140 interviews with him droit de Staline* [*Conversations with Molotov: 140 Interviews with Stalin's Right-Hand Man*]. Paris: Albin Michel, 1995.

Thurston, Robert W. *Life and Terror in Stalin's Russia, 1934-1940.* Yale University Press, 1996.

Tottle, Douglas. *Fraud, Famine, and Fascism: The Ukrainian Genocide Myth from Hitler to Harvard*. Toronto: Progress Books, 1987.

Trotsky, Leon. *Ma Vie* [*My Life*]. Preface by Edwy Plenel. Paris: Édition du Détour, 2019.

Werth, Nicolas. *Le Cimetière de l'espérance* [*The Cemetery of Hope*]. Paris: Tempus Perrin, 2019.

Wolton, Thierry. *Histoire mondiale du communisme. I. Les bourreaux, II. Les victimes, III. Les complices* [*World History of Communism. I. The Executioners. II. The Victims. III. The Accomplices*]. Paris: Grasset, 2015-2017.

Zemskov, Viktor N. "К вопросу о масштабах репресссий в СССCP." Социолологичеческие исссследования 9 (1995).

———. "Заключеченнные, спецпоселенцы, ссыльнопоселенцы, ссыльные и высланны. Стататистико-географичеческий аспект." История СССРР 5 (1991).

———. "Политические репресссии в СССР (1917-1990 гг.)." Росссия XXI 1-2 (1994).

Index Nominum

A

B

C

D

K

L

M

N

O

P

R

S

T

W

Y

Z

Milton Keynes UK
Ingram Content Group UK Ltd.
UKHW040710200824
447134UK00021B/494

9 798330 262090